The
Deepest
Spiritual
Life

The Deepest Spiritual Life

The Art of Combining Personal Spiritual Practice with Religious Community

SUSAN QUINN

WHITE CLOUD PRESS
Ashland, Oregon

First printing: 2002

Cover design by David Ruppe, Impact Publications

Printed in Malaysia

LIBRARY OF CONGRESS CATALOGING-IN-PUBLICATION DATA
Quinn, Susan, 1949-
      The deepest spiritual life : the art of combining personal spiritual
practice with religious community / Susan Quinn.
      p.   cm.
   ISBN: 1-883991-44-7 (pbk.)
   1. Spiritual life I. Title

   BL624. Q54 2002
   291.4'4--dc21
                                                        2002072350

10 9 8 7 6 5 4 3 2 1

CONTENTS

Introduction:
Finding Your Way

There is a moment when we realize that something is not quite right, that we somehow have not been given the whole story, that there is something more to this life than what people seem to think, or what we've been told. The moment that thought arises, we have done what is called "raising the bodhi mind," the aspiration for enlightenment. The moment you do that, the moment that happens, the whole process is complete. This is a process beyond time and space. And it is the birth potential for all sentient beings. ~ John Daido Loori, Sensei, *The Eight Gates of Zen*

We drove down the dusty road until it ended, and found our- selves surrounded by pine trees and silence. As we stepped out of the car, the cool March air greeted us, and although I'd never been to Zen Mountain Center before, I felt like I'd come home. Connie and I left our gear in the car, and we trudged up the path to find out where to put our belongings. I could feel myself smil- ing, free of my usual anxiety about encountering new places. A comfort and certainty of purpose filled my heart, and I sensed my life had begun to change.

After practicing Zen Buddhism for several years, I reflected in 1997 on my spiritual growth and realized that my life had changed profoundly; I found that I was relating to the world with less fear, more compassion and with the ability to understand the nature of my own suffering. There was no doubt in my mind that this emerging transformation could be attributed to my work with Zen, and it was the combination of the spiritual practice and religious community that synergistically expanded my sense of Spirit and connection to those around me. I also knew that there was nothing "magic" about Zen enriching my life; there had to be universal implications: I intuitively believed that there were other religions with spiritual leaders and practitioners who knew the profundity and richness that could be experienced in life by merging the traditional religious life with individual spiritual practices, and who supported others who wanted to embark on this personal journey. I just needed to find them.

In the Beginning

My spiritual journey began with my first Zen experience at Zen Mountain Center in Idyllwild, California. I was a member of a Board of Directors of organization development professionals, and a couple of colleagues had suggested the board go on retreat and see what we thought of the practice of meditation, how it might apply to our work, and whether we might offer the retreat experience to our membership. On the surface, I was intrigued and eager to go; it sounded like an adventure, shades of the mystical and profound; at the same time, I felt drawn to the retreat for other reasons: in spite of how well life was going, I felt an emptiness continually nagging at my consciousness. I was married to a loving and supportive man, work was going well, I had wonderful friends, we had a lovely home . . . and yet life was somehow incomplete. I was so ignorant of Zen that I didn't realize that Zen was an adjective describing a type of Buddhism. Whether that would have affected my decision to go on the retreat, I'll never know.

That weekend changed my life. Now, even after nine years of Zen practice, I wonder at the impact it has had on my life. After learning how to meditate at the retreat, beginning with only five minutes of meditation at a time, I progressed to 15 minutes after returning home, then twenty. After a year of zazen (which is Zen meditation) and sitting 30 minutes per day, I decided to work with a Zen teacher. Eventually I chose to work with a different teacher who had a Zen center in Vista, CA, and she has encouraged me, consoled me, and challenged me in my efforts to mature spiritually. Our eclectic Zen community has also provided me with friendships, and nurtured my personal growth.

Going Home

When I decided to write this book, I knew that I would need to interview people from a variety of religious practices. Since it was obvious to me that Zen offered this type of spiritual life, I decided to find people to interview in the next most familiar territory for me: Judaism. I had been raised a Jew but with only limited exposure to traditional Jewish practice. I guess you could have called me a secular Jew: I believed in God and considered myself a Jew, but was not actively practicing. I decided to speak to a few rabbis and get their feedback on my initial, evolving premise for the book, which narrowly focused on defining a contemplative practice. One of my first interviews in November of 1997 was with Rabbi Jonathan Omer-Man of the Metivta Center for Contemplative Judaism. I didn't know when I first scheduled the interview that he was internationally known and, in fact, had been invited by the Dalai Lama with a contingent of rabbis to have a dialogue regarding the survival of the Jews in the Diaspora. My husband accompanied me to the interview with the rabbi, out of curiosity and to take pictures.

When I met with Rabbi Omer-Man, I told him that I was focused on trying to define "contemplative," which I believed was the key component to my own spiritual development; after a brief discussion and going over my list of questions, he told me, simply, that I wasn't asking the right questions. Not easily deterred, I asked him what the "right questions" were. Rabbi Omer-Man patiently stated, "You need to do more research." We chatted for a while longer, and I pressed him about the homework he thought I needed to do. I told him that I felt compelled to write this book; I just wanted to know where to begin. He said, "Compulsion is the most important thing because it will get you over Rabbi Omer-Man's saying 'start all over again.'" I laughed, agreed, and said, "I realize that I may hit lots of roadblocks." He responded, "And roadblocks can become springboards."

He suggested, for starters, that I read the works of Jack Kornfield, Ken Wilber, Rabbi David Cooper, Thich Nhat Hanh and Matthew Fox, representatives of a wide variety of religions and worldviews. I had already read work by Kornfield and Hanh, but decided to re-read them, not for pleasure but as a researcher, and I decided to read other works by them, too. Later that day my husband and I went straight to the Bodhi Tree Bookstore in Los Angeles and left with an armload of books.

Meanwhile, I also learned from the rabbi that there was a contemplative practice of Judaism that I had never known existed. He mentioned an upcoming Jewish Meditation Conference sponsored by Metivta and other Jewish organizations. In December 1997 I attended the conference. Sitting through several panel discussions and workshops, I was deeply moved by the richness of practice that everyone was describing, and I realized how desperately I was missing a relationship with God. But how could I pursue Judaism when I had become a Buddhist? From a Buddhist perspective, there was no conflict in my also practicing Judaism; although Zen does not speak about God, it is very inclusive of other practices. I knew, however, that eventually I would experience conflicts from a Jewish perspective if I continued my Buddhist practice. I wasn't deterred: I wanted God in my life, and my Jewish heritage was calling me to prayer.

Several months later, trying to be as certain as I could about my aspirations for a Jewish spiritual practice, I decided to begin a Jewish prayer life while maintaining my Zen practice. By that time I had done more research for the book, and its true purpose began to emerge: to explore how for many people, a deeper spiritual life may be discovered through a combination of communal religion and individual spiritual practice. I began to reformulate my list of questions, modifying them every so often based on the responses of the people whom I had begun to interview. I realized it was also time to go back for a visit with Rabbi Omer-Man to ask him about beginning a formal prayer practice, and to ask him about my refined purpose and questions. I had avoided going back to him, nervously wondering if this erudite spiritual leader would validate that I was finally on track. In one sense, I knew I could move ahead without his "approval"; however, I also respected his intellect, spiritual integrity and candor, and knew I would benefit from his feedback.

On a Monday morning, I stopped in to see the rabbi. After he greeted me, I told him about my desire to begin formal prayer, and he recommended I purchase an Artscroll Siddur (Jewish prayer book) and begin by simply reading through the prayers at random; he said I might be surprised at the beauty of the prayers I would find. After that brief discussion, I asked him if he would again look at my list of interview questions for the book; he agreed to review them. I felt my anxiety grow, as I watched him; he quietly took the list, turned to face the window, and read the questions slowly. Before he even turned back to me, he said, "These are wonderful questions," and then quietly repeated his comment. I breathed a sigh of relief and delight, and I knew then that I was on a journey from which I would not, could not, turn back.

Language and Definitions

Let's get some definitions cleared up before we go any further. For the purposes of this book, spirituality encompasses both religious and spiritual practices. Religious practices are those activities that occur in religious communities, which follow particular doctrine, belief systems, rituals and values. Spiritual practices are those activities which guide and assist people in making a more intimate connection with the Divine or universal; these practices can include, but are not limited to, prayer, meditation, journaling, fasting, chant and dance.

Most of the people I interviewed practiced religions that were God-centered, but not all of them. In particular, Buddhism does not address the existence of God, although some Buddhists believe in God and pray. This difference in belief could have created a conflict in the book's language, particularly when describing the ultimate purpose of practice, which is experiencing intimacy with God or the universal. It could be argued by some that "God" and "the universal" are the same; it could also be argued that they are different. I have decided not to debate these terms. At times, based on the language that seems context-appropriate I will use "God" or a substitute for God such as the Divine; at other times I will use "the universal." At still other times, I will use both terms, or "the Infinite One," or "Spirit," or "the All," which could be argued as a term for both. I only request that you not let your biases or personal belief system about God or the absence of God cloud your interest in, and understanding of, this book's purpose: to help you explore what it means to develop a profound spiritual life.

Purpose

Many people are suffering, are sensing the incompleteness of their lives, because they live a superficial existence without meaning or purpose. They sense their estrangement from life, from the Divine, but they have no idea what to do about it. Some of these people may only belong to religions without individual practices, or they may have individual meditative or contemplative practices without belonging to religious community; some of them have no commitment to spirituality in their lives at all. My belief is that for many people, neither religious practices nor spiritual practices are enough, independently, to fill the yearning for an intimate connection with the Divine or universal. There's no doubt in my mind that there are those people who only practice religion or those who only have an individual spiritual practice who have filled their "soul space"; however, most of us need the combination of both religious and spiritual practices to experience a rich and profound spiritual life, revealing the meaning and purpose of our being. I therefore embarked on the journey of finding people who supported this premise, from the standpoint of belief, practice and experience.

The People

To find out more about the meaning and value of combining the gifts of religious community with a personal spiritual practice, I decided to interview people from a number of religious traditions to get as broad and deep a collection of ideas as possible. Conducting the interviews was a delight! I met people from the Episcopal, Jewish, Muslim, Catholic, United Methodist, Science of Mind, nondenominational Christian, Quaker, Presbyterian, Lutheran, Buddhist, and Hindu faith traditions. Some of these people were shy or private, and others were more open and disclosing. Many of them told me about their histories that often included deep physical or emotional pain; others saw their lives as quite ordinary. Some were religious community leaders; others were practitioners. Some were trained spiritual directors; others were not. What they all had in common was their passionate belief in the importance of combining the communal religious and individual spiritual lives. Although many said this path was not for everyone, no one doubted that for many, the deepest spiritual life wedded the communal with the personal.

I began locating people to interview by asking people whom I knew for potential interviewees; at other times I saw people featured in newspaper articles whom I thought would be good subjects. Those early interviewees often suggested other people to be interviewed. Although some people were cautious initially about who I was and how I would represent them and their ideas, most of them, thankfully, realized that I was sincere, open to their input, and respectful, and they were very forthcoming. Most interviews lasted at least one to 1.5 hours, and some of the people I interviewed early in the process consented to follow-up interviews so that I could explore certain questions in more depth. I was moved to discover that although nearly everyone was committed to a specific religious practice, there was rarely criticism of other religious practices; when someone criticized any aspect of religion or spiritual practice, he or she did not direct comments at a specific religion, but rather at the extreme, detrimental or limited use of a particular practice. Those rare people who were critical of other religions (often reflecting their ignorance rather than educated, substantive and objective judgment) are not included in this book.

Limitations

This book is not meant to be a treatise on every aspect of religious and spiritual practices. Since there are many good books available that describe the religions referred to in this book, I have not included extensive descriptions of religions; instead, books on many aspects of religious and spiritual practices are listed in the bibliography at the back of this book. Many spiritual practices, although often originating in one religion, have broader applications for use within other religions. For this reason, a number of spiritual practices from many religious traditions are described in this book.

I have also refused to judge, criticize or recommend any religion that is included in this book. Although I include a number of personal stories from both a Jewish and Zen Buddhist perspective, those stories are meant to illustrate the spiritual qualities and difficulties of my life, rather than recommend that anyone become a Jew or Buddhist. Each person will find that certain religions and spiritual practices "speak to them"; those are the paths they should explore.

I hope that my personal stories reflect the joy and wonder I continually experience as I pursue my spiritual journey. The order of chapters moves from the concrete and specific, to the more profound and transformative; I believe that they are best read in order, but also believe that each chapter can stand on its own. Chapter 1 explains the nature of the current spiritual revival that is taking place; Chapter 2 describes the importance and benefits of participating in religious community, and what is missing if you don't have a personal practice; Chapter 3 explains the reasons for pursuing an individual spiritual practice, and what is missing if you don't participate in religious community; Chapter 4 illustrates what it means to merge a religious and spiritual practice; Chapter 5 explains the type of commitment that a religious/spiritual practice requires; Chapter 6 defines the role of a spiritual guide and where to find one; Chapter 7 explains how serving others deepens one's spiritual life; Chapter 8 addresses the questions that a religious/spiritual practice answers; Chapter 9 describes how a religious/spiritual practice clarifies one's purpose and changes one's life; and Chapter 10 provides suggestions for creating your own spiritual path. Even if you read the chapters at random, you will likely find that reading the book in its entirety will give you a more complete picture of what it can mean to lead a spiritual life.

Ultimately only you can decide whether the quality of your inner life is sufficient to move you to pursue a spiritual practice and religious community; sometimes your pain has to be greater than the fear or reluctance to begin the journey. I hope that this book will provide you with the motivation and impetus to explore your own spiritual path; the decision to discover intimacy with God or being one with the universe is a yearning seed, sleeping within your soul, only waiting to be awakened.

Chapter One

Why Spiritual Revival Now?

It may be that the mechanization of our industrial environment—steel sheets and girders, concrete piers and asphalt roads, belching blast furnaces, heavy coal smoke and dead neon signs—it may be that this enveloping insentience has led us unconsciously to assume that all environments are inanimate, whereas in fact, of course, above the smog the stars still shine and the angels sing. If deep is answering to deep less today it is not because the depths have changed, certainly not on their objective side. If our world has changed, this only reflects the change in the idea we now have of it. God has not retreated; it is we who have turned away. ~ HUSTON SMITH, *Forgotten Truth*

A*spiritual awakening is happening.* Of those I interviewed, no one doubted that we were all witnessing a spiritual revival. Periods of spiritual awakening are not new to human history, but the historic reasons for the revival, the current social reasons and the personal reasons for seeking a spiritual life are driven by the conditions of modernism and people's growing awareness that rationalism and materialism do not fill one's soul space.

To understand the spiritual revival of the 1990s we first need to look at the impact of the period of Enlightenment [17th–18th

centuries]that moved us away from spirituality and toward secularism. We'll discuss the social conditions that have developed in the absence of spiritual depth, and the limited ability of traditional mainstream religion to help people develop a personal spiritual life; and we'll look at how the lack of a spiritual life has led people to try to fill their soul space with all kinds of destructive alternatives, only to find that they still hunger for that which they do not understand, recognize or know how to find: the essence of Spirit.

Historic Reasons

With the Enlightenment, we entered a period that celebrated the rational and scientific approach to life. As Wade Clark Roof stated, this period ". . . privileged mind over body, technology over nature, innovation over tradition, knowledge over experience, mastery over mystery." We entered a secular age, during which, as Sister Jane DeLisle, Executive Director of the Center for Spiritual Development says, "We made science and knowledge sacred, and negated the inner soul of each person." Although mainstream religions continued to function post-Enlightenment, they were seen as illogical and irrational, and viewed, at the very least, as irrelevant by some, and as threatening to an orderly, technologically advancing world by others. That isn't to say that modernism and science haven't made enormous contributions to our lives, to our very existence, but the gains came at a high price: we essentially lost our souls to the doctrine of progress.

Because many believed in, and found solace in, a world that is orderly, predictable and logical, they denied or avoided exploring the possibility of a spiritual existence, living and embracing a life of mystery, acknowledging the unknowable, and exploring the profundity and unexplainable presence of Spirit. Logic, reason and a desire for orderliness did not deepen their spiritual lives, however; many felt empty, alone and bereft. These were the conditions leading into this century.

Today, the statistical information on spiritual revival is admittedly paradoxical and contradictory, making it nearly impossible to draw conclusions based on the data: books on spirituality are the fastest growing segment of the publishing market, yet church attendance could be holding steady, increasing or declining, depending on the survey you read. Cecile Holmes in the *Houston Chronicle* (2/23/00), noted the following statistics from the book, *Surveying the Religious Landscrape:Trends in U.S. Beliefs*, by George Gallup written with D. Michael Lindsay: more than 80% of Americans desire to grow spiritually, and church and synagogue attendance has remained relatively steady over the past 50 years. In contrast, the Ontario Consultants on Religious Tolerance published a paper on its website (www.religioustolerance.org) that referenced several surveys which put attendance at church between 25% and 41%; however, the paper also suggested that Americans inflated these numbers when surveyed. In addition, while traditional religions are seeing declines in attendance, evangelical and charismatic churches are among the fastest growing congregations. Since there are conflicting data and patterns regarding the premise that a spiritual revival is taking place, I have relied on the perceptions of those I interviewed, as well as drawn my own conclusions.

Social Reasons

I grew up in a predominantly secular household. Although we attended high holiday services and I went to "Sunday school," and to Hebrew school (taught after regular school hours twice a week), my parents seldom spoke about Judaism and I never felt moved to pursue a spiritual life. I enjoyed learning Hebrew, and even could have been Bat Mitzvah'ed (my parents gave me the choice), the Jewish equivalent of the rite of passage from childhood to adulthood; I decided against the ritual because it seemed like more of a "thing to do," than an opportunity for spiritual development.

Eventually, the baby boomers (with me in their midst) rebelled in the 1960s, where values identified with parents were abandoned, literally and/or figuratively, depending on one's level of rebelliousness. I was an ambivalent, closet rebel, and cruised through much of that period without creating a stir; I was not prepared to abandon the order and structure that I was deluded into thinking was the basis of a meaningful existence. Although I wasn't particularly happy, I was "doing the right things": getting good grades, keeping out of trouble, and making reasonable plans for the foreseeable future. During this period, I even studied in Israel for one year, and although it stimulated my interest in, and study of, Judaism, I still felt remote from my spiritual roots. Once I entered the 1970s, I'd found the love of my life, who, although not Jewish, was supportive of the religious activities that I wanted to pursue, which were pretty much limited to the haphazard observance of Hanukah and Passover. Those activities defined the extent of my spiritual practices. Materialism became my god, but houses, nice cars, and expensive vacations did not assuage my spiritual hunger. Life, on the whole, was good, but the nagging hint that something was amiss never went away.

It never occurred to me that a Jewish community might help me rediscover my lost spirit, but quite frankly, most synagogues would only have been able to help with one side of spirituality, as I define it: formal religion and community; the resources for developing a personal spiritual practice were, and still are, difficult to find in mainstream Judaism. That limitation is not unique to Judaism. Wade Clark Roof says the following about Protestantism:

> ... mainstream Protestant churches have so accommodated modernity by emphasizing creed and doctrine that they have lost the depth and experiential dimensions—emotion, feelings, soul. This loss is compounded by a serious disjuncture between the private and public realms of experience within the more liberal theological traditions, thereby eroding their ability to engage the culture and to sustain a vision of wholeness. Indeed, the revolt against organized religion by many young Americans since the 1960s might be viewed as essentially a reaction to this loss of unity and inwardness."

So for many, the institutions that could provide both the moral foundation and belief systems, as well as the opportunity for developing a personal spiritual life, fell short of the mark.

Today, people are watching others begin their own independent spiritual journeys, and they want to know what that might mean for them. The Reverend Murray Finck, the Bishop of the Pacifica Synod, Evangelical Lutheran Church in America says,

> There are many people connected with the institutional church who are watching other people, sometimes their own family members, their

children, neighbors, friends, co-workers, heading off on a spiritual journey that doesn't have much to do with the church; they're questioning why their church or synagogue or religious institutions aren't meeting that need, and wondering what's drawing people toward other religious expressions. Then they become curious and want to know what's missing in their own religious community that is supposed to meet all of their spiritual needs, and why people are going to other communities to develop a deeper sense of personal spirituality. I think people are simply looking for a more holistic approach to a spiritual life.

Father John McAndrew, Parochial Vicar of St. Angela Merici Church in Brea, California comments, "My perception is that people are spiritual. Somebody once said, 'I'm not a human being trying to have a spiritual life; I'm a spiritual being trying to live a human life.' There is a perception, however, that post-Enlightenment, we have separated out the spiritual and the sacred, the supernatural and the natural, and there is this great divide; I think one of the tasks of modern spirituality is to bring that back together."

Personal Pain

In this new century, for many the personal pain of spiritual deprivation has reached a new high. Not only baby boomers are experiencing the desolation of spirit; Generation X, the first generation to be raised without *any* type of religious foundation, has also been desperately searching for answers. Since materialism has failed to fulfill people's personal aspirations for wholeness, they have developed "addictions" to fill the void. Materialism has been an unsuccessful plan of acquisitiveness pursued to satisfy the unbearable, inexplicable internal yearning. With the realization that satisfaction may not be coming from their exterior lives, people have now turned self-destructive, inadvertently destroying their own bodies, desecrating the temple of their souls: over-eating, alcoholism, drug addiction and sex dominate the lives of many who struggle to lessen the pain of their existence, acting as if they need to pacify or even destroy a ravenous monster within, when it's the soul crying out for sustenance. Instead of recognizing spirit that ever waits to be acknowledged and embraced, self-destructive behaviors are pursued, in a relentless effort to stop the pain.

Sensei Nicolee Miller-McMahon notes the pain people experience as they experience incessant change: "I feel that we have a sense of rapid change that is so overwhelming, that frankly I think people are returning to communal religion because it offers more of a safe haven; it gives some certainty, some structure and form to these rapidly changing times." Trying to grasp the vastness of potential change can be both inspiring and staggering at the same time.

Pastor Preston Price echoes the impact of change: "We are living in a very different kind of world, things are changing so radically, and to many that's disconcerting; nothing is dependable and the only constant is change. So the search for some kind of ground or center becomes even more important."

Charlotte Cleghorn, an Episcopal priest, believes Carl Jung's premise, that "the first half of life is a time of developing ego, career, having kids, which supposedly makes you who you are, but the second half of life is asking the deeper questions: what is life about, who am I and who are you, and where does this all come from?"

What characterizes the emerging spiritual revival is a change in one question being asked; instead of continually inquiring, "what will it take to feed me?" people are beginning to ask, "what needs to be fed?" When they ask that question, soul can respond, and spirit answers.

Spiritual Signs

Somehow I avoided the many self-destructive addictive behaviors that others pursued; it would be difficult for me to guess the reasons why. For one, in spite of my lack of a committed spiritual practice, I always felt the presence of, and believed in, God. I also had developed a strong sense of values and personal discipline. When I discovered Zen Buddhism, it gave me the framework for developing my own spirituality: to begin to fill the emptiness, to find ways to work with constant change, and to clarify the meaning of my life. In my moments of meditative silence, I felt more than ever the closeness of God; at times when I wasn't meditating, I often perceived God's presence and discovered a new ability to understand my own life and my relationship with others. I began to understand the nature of my own suffering and the suffering of others, while developing a growing sense of compassion for and empathy with those around me. With my renewed connection with God, I felt the need to pray and meditate on God's presence; at that point I felt moved to re-connect with my Jewish roots. If I was going to pray to God, I wanted to pray within a Jewish context.

My eclectic approach to spirituality is not unique. Wade Clark Roof has done extensive research on contemporary spiritual seekers and includes the following aspects in his profile of them:

- They are highly individualistic and consumption oriented, inclined to select for themselves what they will believe or practice . . .
- They frequently subscribe to a multi-layered or pastiche-style spirituality that mixes and matches elements from a variety of religious traditions, chosen more for their experiential than their objective-truth value and for their ability to help one to grow as a person . . .
- They often move from one spiritual exploration to another, giving the impression of being more interested in the journey than in the destination.[1]

Although there are benefits to incorporating aspects of different practices in one's spiritual life, there are also limitations. Clark's description gives me the impression that people are seeking, but have not found a way to ground themselves by committing to community. Although there is much to learn by exploring many religious and spiritual practices, and in fact much to gain by being creative in developing personal spiritual practices, ultimately I have benefited most by choosing a primary religious practice and community, which at this time is Zen Buddhism. My own journey reflects this research on contemporary religious life. I have not abandoned my Jewish roots, and I continue to incorporate aspects of Judaism into my personal spiritual life. And I read widely about religion. But my spiritual home is now Zen Buddhism. Choosing a community and a path is important. As Rabbi Omer-Man once said to me, "At some point one has to choose

---

1.   Wade Clark Roof, "Modernity, the Religious, and the Spiritual" in *Annals of the American Academy of Political and Social Science*, July 1998, p. 211.

one's practice." Later in this book I will explain the benefits of "grounding" oneself in a religious community, while being more flexible in experimenting with different activities for one's personal spiritual practice.

What Do We Seek?

Most of us are suffering in some way, and are simply looking for a way to get rid of the pain, rather than pursuing spirituality for lofty reasons. Some of the reasons people pursue a spiritual life are the following:

1) People seek spiritual lives that make them feel good, that perpetually help them transcend the tedium of a mundane existence. Much of the energy around spiritual revival may have to do with those people who hope that spirituality will make their lives more fun, happy, interesting and stimulating.

2) People are looking for formulas. In some ways, religious communities provide "formulas" for developing a spiritual life; every religion has doctrine and spiritual laws that outline how people should act and treat each other, and these moral and ethical principles are essential to developing a spiritual path. But people also want formulas that will lead them to enlightenment or liberation; they want the steps to be easy, simple, and fast. I was at one retreat where a woman was very disappointed that she had still not experienced enlightenment, which she felt entitled to after one year of dedicated meditation! Many people give up on spirituality because they aren't getting results fast enough.

3) People want a spiritual practice that is pain-free. This is the other side of seeking a life of happiness and highs. A spiritual life, which *is* your very life, encompasses everything: pain and fear, joy and beauty, laughter and tears. It sometimes causes us to face the darkest parts of ourselves as well as the beauty of our lives. Spiritual practice is not always painful, and in fact is often joyful, and it teaches us who we really are. That's hard work.

So if our spiritual aspirations are self-centered or idealistic, should we just give them up? Is there something wrong with us? Not at all. But at some point, we need to recognize that spirituality serves both a higher and deeper purpose. A religious/spiritual life does not rid us of the ordinariness of living; it helps us to find profundity, beauty and richness *within the ordinary*. Although a side benefit of practice might be an occasional high, we don't so much transcend life or get high on spirituality; rather, a spiritual life helps us find our meaning and purpose within existence, reminds us of our calling to elevate, or to save or to liberate ourselves and others from the illusions of how we wish life could be, and celebrate and rejoice in the experience that is right in front of us. A religious/spiritual life shows us that although the Divine may seem distant and inexplicable, It is also available to us in every moment.

And so spiritual revival is occurring. Its manifestation may not be orderly or conventional and its motivations may not always be elevated or profound. But for those of us who are on the path, our seeking to find a way to ground ourselves within community, as well as elevate ourselves within a personal spiritual practice, can provide the context for and nurturing of a rich and purposeful spiritual life.

CHAPTER TWO

Why Pursue A Religious Practice?

Once Rabbi Bunam was praying at an inn. People jostled and pushed him, but he did not go into his room. Later he said to his disciples, "Sometimes it seems impossible to pray in a certain place and one seeks out another place. But that is not the right thing to do. For the place we have quitted cries out mournfully: Why did you refuse to make your devotions here with me? If you met with obstacles, it was a sign that it was up to you to redeem me." ~ MARTIN BUBER, *Tales of the Hasidim*

I should try telling my friends who have a hard time comprehending why I like to spend so much time going to church with Benedictines that I do so for the same reasons that I write: to let words work the earth of my heart. ~ KATHLEEN NORRIS, *The Cloister Walk*

---

*A*s I finish taking one last look at the waffles in the oven, I make my way toward the zendo where service is being held. I have missed half of the ceremony, but I am the cook for breakfast and the importance of those responsibilities supersedes the need for my presence at service. The cook is the one who feeds the community, who provides the basic sustenance that everyone requires. As I approach the zendo, I hear the chanting and stop in my tracks. Ordinarily when I participate in the chanting, I am immersed in *the world of words and sounds. But suddenly I am a listener, an observer, a voyeur; I slowly approach the zendo and am moved by the ancient words, voices, sounds and rhythms that echo the stories and lives of the ancient past. I hear the intoning of monks in India, in Tibet, in Japan, in China; they are the very same voices that drum and vibrate only footsteps away. I stand quietly for a moment, letting the sounds enter my body and mind. For an instant I am witnessing the coupling between past and present. Then I quietly enter the zendo and allow my voice to merge with the music of the infinite.*

Religious Practice

Religious practice gives us the opportunity to connect, and become grounded in, traditions that often have ancient roots, or have developed belief systems linked to olden wisdoms and practices. For the purposes of this book, religious practice is defined as those activities that occur in religious communities that follow particular doctrine, belief systems, rituals and values. Each religion has its own belief systems; some have dogma, some don't. Some have ancient rituals that are practiced today to evoke one's awareness of Spirit in every day life; others are austere, still others are more contemporary. Although religions may differ in their manifestation of practice, they all have one thing in common: community. If we see community as the environment for religious practice, it is the place where we experience Spirit and are supported by others in the diverse and rich practices that contribute to a spiritual life. So community is where we start.

Community

The irony of our times is that many of us avoid community, particularly religious community, for a myriad of reasons. Some people have had traumatic or disappointing experiences with organized religion; some people feel they don't have enough time to devote to religion or are unwilling to give the little free time they have to religious community. Others see religions as restrictive, unimaginative or superficial, because they haven't discovered the religious groups that can meet their hopes and expectations for community.

Religious communities can also be hotbeds of political strife. Cliques form, dividing those who are "in" and those who are "out." I've heard stories of in-fighting, and many of us have heard of the reprehensible behavior of lay and religious leaders. All of these reflect the difficulties that can wound, even destroy, any community, and religious communities are not immune to these faults and limitations. I think it is also fair to hold religious communities to a higher standard than other organizations. Yet the epidemic of isolation that people suffer from in these times is almost palpable. When people reach out to one another in religious community, in an environment that guides, teaches, comforts and reassures them, they seek to transform the isolation that permeates their lives. Religious practice in a community that complements their aspirations for a spiritual life provides the opportunity for them to transcend their loneliness and discover a spirituality that enriches and guides their soul's journey.

So what do we do when we find our community is becoming mired in pettiness, or leaders are mistreating or violating community members' trust? We can keep our distance and judge and criticize; or we can leave and seek another community that meets our ideals; or we can act courageously by working within the community to call attention to its pettiness and politics, or misbehaviors or violations. These are the times when we put our spirituality into real, practical and compassionate practice. When we examine how a religious practice helps us on our journey, lifting us from our isolation and calling us to serve others in courageous ways, we begin to understand how it becomes a critical component of the spiritual path.

Relationship

Religious practice provides us with community, and by participating in community, we have the opportunity to be in relationship with others pursuing the same path, transcending the isolation that is so much a factor in every day life. The Rev. Charlotte Cleghorn, an Episcopal priest and spiritual director, explains how Paul, a disciple of Jesus, described community: "Paul compares the Christian community to the human body; he talks about the different parts of the body and how they need to be together. If everything were an ear, how would we see, and if everything were an eye, how would we speak? All these different parts of the body make it one, just as there are different kinds of people with different gifts. In community, they bring those gifts together. When members of the body are missing, the body is diminished." When we develop relationships with others, we experience what it means to be connected to others, and we provide the connectedness that others need, too.

When we connect with other people, we learn the joys of giving and receiving. Sister Jane DeLisle, Executive Director of the Center for Spiritual Development, talks about the importance of sharing our gifts: "Whatever a person has or does, or whatever graces are received by a loving God—those gifts are not just for the person; they're to be shared with the community, the common good. That's important." When we recognize our gifts, we realize that we don't "own" them, but rather that they are spiritual offerings we've received that we can most appreciate when others benefit from them, too. There is a reciprocity of joy and relatedness that occurs when we share our gifts with others.

In community we have the opportunity to make our scattered lives whole by pursuing a celebration of life with others. We can be supported by others who, paradoxically, are of like mind in the quest of pursuing a spiritual path, yet who hold diverse perspectives about the meaning of the journey, people who understand the challenges of leading a spiritual life. When we struggle, others can comfort us. When we rejoice, others can share our joy and celebrate with us. When we get off track, not living lives that reflect our higher selves, they can remind us of whom we aspire to be. When we question our path, everyone has his or her own way to encourage us: a person may share a similar struggle; another may find just the right words to empathize or reassure us; yet another might comfort us with humor and lightness. We have found a support group of diverse individuals who share our basic values and beliefs. And as others have their times of struggle with life's disappointments and trials, we can return the gift of being a spiritual friend to them, too.

In our Zen community, we have a wonderful collection of participants. Our ages range from the 20s to the 80s; some of us are just beginning our adult lives and our spiritual journeys, and others have volumes of experiences that would take a lifetime to share. Some of us are extroverts, others are introverts. Some see Zen as a practical pursuit, one that helps them reduce their stress; others see Zen as a deeply spiritual pursuit with shades of the mystical. What surprises me is that outside of our shared practice of Zen, many of us would not seek each other out as friends. And yet there are people whom I've known for a long time with whom I don't experience the sense of relatedness and intimacy that I feel within my Zen community. Because we share a spiritual path and know its demands, its rewards, its frustrations and its lessons, we are bonded together in an empathic and devoted way. I deeply admire and appreciate these people who honor my journey and allow me to sustain them in theirs.

I have had some of my greatest lessons in religious community by becoming active on the Board of Directors of my Zen community. As an independent consultant, I spend a great deal of time working on my own and only serving my clients. As a member of the Board, I am tested in my ability to listen to others who may have very different opinions about what best serves the community. I am challenged in my ability to listen empathically and genuinely; I am moved to stand in their shoes, to at least understand their points of view. Sometimes a very task-oriented person, I am reminded that others sometimes simply have a need to be heard, and to have their ideas seriously considered. I am challenged to actualize in a very fundamental way my values and beliefs about relationship, such as compassion and empathy. If I am moved to help my religious community mature and meet its mission, might I not have something to learn from others? Might not their points of view at times be valuable and offer more beneficial outcomes than my own?

In religious community, I think we have an incomparable opportunity to simply witness the circumstances of others. Many of the people I interviewed spoke of the importance of listening, particularly listening to God. If I can't listen to others, how in the world will I ever be able to listen to God, to truly hear God? Religious practice gives me a chance to do just that: practice listening, practice being present and open to the ideas, concerns, dreams and goals of others, to open to the Divine that exists in each person. If others are less skilled than I am at listening, I can choose to judge, criticize or abandon them. Or I can model appropriate listening behaviors through my willingness and ability to be available to them as they struggle to be heard and understood. My personal choices about relating to others in these situations speak volumes about my spiritual evolution and my willingness to grow, my eagerness to expand my perception of possibilities and learn that which is new. Relating to others in religious community forces me, encourages me, comforts me, challenges me to reach out to others, to serve them and be served by them, in our efforts to break down barriers and see ourselves as the one body of Spirit.

Relationship in religious community can also provide solace for those who feel isolated or alone. As Nicolee Jikyo Miller-McMahon, Sensei of the Three Treasures Zen Community says, "We live in a pretty disenfranchised culture, and we don't have family around, yet our connections with others can come in different ways. Religious communities can offer that connection; they can't take the place of family, but they can be a place of soul nurturing." Van Pewthers, Christian pastor, provides another perspective: "In relationship with God, we come into a true understanding of not only who we are but what we were created for, and because of those two things, we have the possibility of having relationship in community with others who are similarly moving in the same direction."

Community can help us define who we are. Rabbi Wayne Dosick of the Elijah Minyan explains the role of the Jewish community in this way:

> The institution defines the parameters of the quest. So in Judaism, the institution creates community; it inspires us to do mitzvahs (good deeds), it inspires us to support the tripod of God, Torah and Israel, the Jewish people and the Jewish land. It creates for us a definition of who we are and who we are not, so Jews for example believe God is one and not three, that we're each responsible for our own actions, all those kinds of theological issues. In many ways, we are defined much beyond those terms, because Judaism is not only a religion; it's a peoplehood,

so we have a shared history, we have a shared language, a shared land, a shared literature, a shared culture, a shared destiny. So all of those things go into nationhood, ethnicity, the kinds of things that link us as a people.

In relationship with others in religious community, we learn how to not only emulate but *live* the spiritual life. The community mirrors for us those areas where we are most stuck, where we are determined to be right, where we are committed to looking good above all else. Sometimes in religious community we begin to think that our "take" on religious practice is better or more correct than another person's. We compare our religious practice to others, justifying (even if only to ourselves) that we are more pious, more devoted, more knowledgeable, more charitable—more of anything that would make us superior to others. By practicing in religious community, we have the opportunity to learn, over and over again, that we are all on the same journey, sharing similar goals and aspirations, struggling with the same concepts and teachings, each of us with our own strengths and limitations, needs and contributions; that there is no competition for being more righteous or superior, except in our own minds. When we actively participate in religious community, we have many opportunities to remember that we are all on the same spiritual path, together.

I can't believe that no one has done anything yet! For two days of this meditation retreat I have listened to one woman in our midst who is continually in motion: she moves her legs, scrapes her feet on the floor, clears her throat repeatedly, scoots around on her chair—why she's even noisily reached down for her water bottle, popped open the plastic top and had a swig! In this silent Jewish retreat, I am certain that I can't be the only one who has written a note of complaint to the rabbi. I tried to be compassionate in my note, explaining that I know how difficult it must be for the woman to sit quietly, but couldn't someone kindly tell her to be still?? I am ruminating about this woman, feeling slightly guilty, for I spoke with her just before the retreat began, and she seemed like a nice person . . . finally this meditation period is ending and the rabbi will be answering some of our questions and concerns. As people stir and settle into their places, the rabbi begins to speak to those of us who complained about the restless participant. "A few of you have written notes to protest the restlessness of others. It is very easy to become distracted and annoyed by what we think others should be doing. I'd suggest you reflect on what your protestations say about yourself and your practice; what can you learn from your reactions to others?" I am chagrined, because I've known all along that he is right. Genuine compassion on my part would have been to realize that sitting quietly in meditation must have been extremely difficult for this woman. My annoyance also spoke to my perception of my superiority in being able to meditate quietly and my need to be right about the proper way to meditate, as well as my desire to have things just the way I wanted them. I feel my anger dissolve into sheepishness, and then relief, as I realize that nothing keeps me from meditating peacefully—except myself . . . I had no problem meditating calmly the remainder of the retreat . . .

Those with whom we are in relationship have much to teach us when we open to the spaciousness of Spirit by considering and re-evaluating our own perspectives; those times when we close ourselves to others and create obstacles to considering the concerns of others due to our fear, anger or selfishness only erect barriers and constrict our learning. Although we have the ability to reflect on the state of our own soul and the actions we take that assist or limit our spiritual development, only through the messages reflected back to us by others can we complete the exploration of who we really are and where we are on the spiritual path.

A Place to Be

At a time when people feel as if they are living lives of chaos, and see no end in sight, religious practice provides a history, a path, a language, a grounding, a framework for living one's life. Religion provides an ethical path for living one's life morally and from a spiritual perspective. Dr. Muzammil Siddiqi, Executive Director of the Islamic Society of Orange County, California explains, "In Islam we have beliefs, laws, a total way of life, called *din*. Prayer five times a day reminds us that we are servants of God, 24 hours a day. Being a Muslim means submitting your life to God, and God becomes the center of your life."

"I believe people are seeking a belief system, something that will shape their own values and beliefs and their moral deliberations, and they are looking for a credible group to help them in that journey," says the Rev. Murray Finck, a Bishop in the Evangelical Lutheran Church in America. "I believe many religious expressions today are helping people to make choices in their everyday life, in how to live a life full of values and a life that is in harmony with God, nature and one another."

Rabbi Jonathan Omer-Man of Metivta describes the purpose of religious practice: "It provides people with a language and a path, lets them know there *is* a language, there *is* a path. Religion provides that path and enriches a person's vocabulary of understanding, where they are going and who is with them."

The Stories

Karen Goran, a spiritual director, speaks of the importance of religious stories: "I think it's important for people to know the stories of their faith. I know people who are struggling, in part because they don't know the important stories, Old or New Testament. So they get held back on the inner journey. If you know the stories, you create a thread between yourself and history." By knowing the stories of our faiths we learn over and over again that the trials that we suffer, the sorrows, the joys, the realizations connect us to a lineage of those who have walked the same path. We remember that, whatever chaos we are experiencing, we are not alone, have never been alone, will never be alone. The path that others have historically walked is the same path we walk today. Father John McAndrew says,

> Community is primarily a narrative—it's a community that has a story to tell. That defining story helps the community to identify itself. That story is traditionally passed on in the Book. For Christians, it was a story that also had deep Jewish roots, so that the Christian tradition

incorporated it; we stole wholesale from our Jewish brothers and sisters large portions of it—our understanding of God, our prayers, our liturgy, our worship—because we understood that that was part of our story, too. So there's *my* story, which is my own human experience, and in the religious community we identify *my* story with *the* story as *our* story, and it becomes a filter of understanding our own experience in the light of this defining story. I think it is also the defining element of the spirituality of the 12 steps in the recovery community of narrative. We're not learning so much educational information about alcoholism as we are learning stories of people's lives that have been shattered and rebuilt. And it's that story that becomes *our* story.

At one time I contemplated the Book of Job from the Old Testament. On the surface, it was a tragic story of one man's struggle with his faith. I remember having difficulty reading the story, mulling over what appeared to be God's test of Job and Job's suffering, and reading the judgmental opinions of men who were supposed to be his friends. But as I worked with the story and related it to my own life, I realized from my own perspective that Job believed he could barter with God; that if he did all the right things, God would pay up by providing him with the good life; that if God loved him, all these difficult events would not be happening. The story refers to the "Adversary" whom God gives permission to "test" Job's faith; to me, Job's adversary was his own arrogance, his thinking that God owed him. He suffered not only from the destruction that befell him, but from his belief that God was being unjust, as if he could comprehend the mind of God. Job's transformation took place when he let go of every single belief and expectation for his life and for God; when he realized that life continually provides us with challenges as our circumstances are ever-changing. I believe God was waiting for Job to realize that he already had everything that he needed in his life, including God's love; that life as it unfolded was truly whole and complete, and that Job's suffering came, not just from the grievous events of his life, but from his expectations of how life should be different.

Although I have had nowhere near the devastation in my life that Job experienced, I was astounded at how Job's suffering was so like my own: that I suffered when I wished things to be other than they were, when I felt entitled to have what I wanted; and that my suffering was relieved, even when life was difficult, when I recognized and embraced my life as full, even when I couldn't always have every desire met.

An example of a contemporary story of Job was shared with me in my interview with Mary Strouse, a practicing Catholic. Mary looked young for her age, petite with short dark hair, and in spite of her physical pain, she glowed with faith and devotion. Much of our conversation was punctuated with her enthusiasm, sincerity and laughter. Mary was recovering from two spinal surgeries in her neck, and her story was deeply moving as she explained how she worked with her condition:

> One time I was trying to understand suffering and doing a meditation on suffering during Lent. I'll never forget one moment when I was getting into the shower, and I was saying, "I still don't understand suffering," and God was asking me if I would suffer for this thing, or if I would suffer for that thing, and I answered "yes" each time. Finally God said, "Would you suffer for a soul?" I had to say "yes," you just have to say yes to that, and the next day my pain came. I've been dealing with this pain and the subsequent recovery from surgery for a while, so I hope that whoever is getting what they need (laughter) is appreciating it . . . it's been a long haul . . . one of the things I had to do was hold on to the fact that this is helping somebody, that God wants this and I will not take my "yes" back. Many times I've been tempted but I will not do it, and that's what helps me through.

So we can connect our own stories of faith to ancient stories in our religious traditions, and our suffering and our transcendence of suffering are a link between a historic lineage of faith and those who will come after us.

Sacred Space

Attending communal religious service is one aspect of religious practice that fills people's needs for community and spirit. The Reverend Lois McAfee, spiritual director says,

> People may need to keep looking until they find a place that says "home" to them. Some of us endure a lot when we go to worship mismatched,

and we don't have the good sense to realize that if one community isn't the place for us to worship, we need to look some more until consolation comes. And we're invited by God to find our faith community, our home. Even though some of us may be most comfortable praying in solitude, we miss something when we don't pray with others. I'm told the word "worship" comes from the Welsh word meaning worth-ship. In good worship, we pause in the course of our daily life to remember our full worth in light of God's full mysterious worth as conveyed in all of the elements of the worship service: those of words and images and, when enough time is allowed, those beyond words and forms, in the fullness of silence.

Nicolee Jikyo Miller-McMahon, Sensei speaks about the place in which we commune: "Sacred space does something in community to open the heart-mind, that's my own experience; I've found that to be true in almost any religious community that I've attended. If I were to go to a church or temple or mosque, there is something special about sacred space where people have been practicing together, or attending services together and hearing talks, and doing that over a long time period. The space carries a quality of sacredness, and when people enter it, it's as if it's a big enough container to carry their pain; it becomes a place of refuge."

As we sit in our places forming a circle on the Sabbath of this Jewish meditation retreat, we are asked who would like to make aliyah, literally going upward, or stepping forward for the reading of the torah. I find my jaw quivering, tears in my eyes, since I have never been invited to make aliyah. The rabbi sits in the center of the larger circle, the torah unrolled before him. We take turns in small, intimate groups approaching the torah; I am in the last group of five or six of us making aliyah (most of us in this group never having done it before); we encircle the rabbi and torah. Those who have prayer shawls put them around those of us who have none. We stand with our arms around each others' shoulders in a gentle embrace that embodies our connectedness stretching over 5,000 years. The rabbi begins the Hebrew prayer that precedes the read-

reading of the torah; I am startled to realize that the words used to respond to the rabbi's invocation are on my own lips; my prayer memories of more than 35 years ago spring forth and I chant them with reverence and gratitude. We sing, pray, respond, celebrate, and listen to the ancient chants that honor our Jewish tradition, illuminate our present, and reveal our future. Shoulder to shoulder we cry, we rejoice, we pray.

Ritual

Within the sacred space, religious practice offers the chance to transcend the ordinary and commune with Spirit in the presence of others. The Rev. Charlotte Cleghorn believes, "The singing of hymns, psalms, prayers, goes deep into people's souls and psyches. People have been known to draw on those things they didn't know were there, when they were in crisis. The other important thing is that in the liturgy we try to use the senses and the whole body; I don't think people are conscious of that: the incense and the bells, the intellect and the senses, the artistic, all contribute to the whole."

Ritual in communal religious practice reminds us that no matter how lonely we may feel, we are never alone. Pastor Preston Price of the United Methodist Church of Garden Grove talks about ritual in this way: "We have done rituals about all sorts of things to help people move psychologically and spiritually through a transition; we have a divorce ceremony, a ceremony for losing a child by miscarriage, for dedications for homes. What's important is the opportunity to act out something symbolic in real time, in real life. It's a chance for you to invite friends and family, those people who have gotten you to this point and who will get you beyond this point. It is a whole body, physical, holistic experience, as we use the senses: smell, taste, touch, sight and sound."

Too often, we think that we can deal with life's challenges only by thinking them through; we believe that if we spend enough time thinking about things we can figure them out. Sometimes, though, I've found that relinquishing my preference to be logical and rational is a chance to enter the spiritual realms in a completely integrated and intuitive way. If I participate in a Zen service, my entire body becomes a part of a shared, collective experience. It is like choreography, and we are all dancers; the beauty of our activity is not just when we do our own thing, but when we focus on every other person, bringing harmony to our activities. Whether we bow, light incense, ring bells, chant, or simply listen, we are part of a synchronized ballet, an artistic, soul-sourced manifestation of spirit. The experience is at once joyful and serious, poignant and fun, individual and communal, predictable and unique.

Life With Meaning

Religious practice gives us the chance to experience and grow through our relationships in community, by providing us with a path we can traverse with others, a belief system that provides us with the values, ethics, history, and rituals that enable us to engage in our practice in a metaphorical and heartfelt way. In addition, religious practice provides us with the potential for learning how to fulfill our purpose in life; it provides us with a means to explore meaning, to understand our mission, to know who we are and why we are here as creatures created to be in relationship. Since our focus in life can be narrowed to fulfilling our baser needs, religions provide the framework for us to rise above our self-centeredness and remember what it means to lead a spiritual life. Rabbi Steve Robbins of Temple N'Vay Shalom explains the purpose of Judaism. "One of the most important parts of Judaism is the combination of form and content, the unification of the two. From the point of view of Judaism, the world is incomplete, unfinished, and our task as beings in God's image is to complete the task of creation." Kay Lindahl spoke of her need to use her gift to listen and speak: "I was at a small conference of 30, and our job was to write an initial draft of a charter for the United Religions Initiative. I found myself listening really intently to what was being said, and *what wanted to be said there*, what was being spoken, and *what wanted to come out of what was being spoken*, so I wasn't talking a lot. I only said something when I was *moved to speak*. The difference has become more apparent—when I'm moved to speak, or when I'm just speaking. Another way I explain it is, 'the voice that I am,' versus 'my voice.' So one of my jobs in life is to listen intently, and then when I "hear" that voice, I speak; that's my gift."

Over time I have become more and more clear about my own purpose in life, although that purpose is an organically emerging, evolving and maturing process. I believe I am here to serve and to teach. The beauty of serving is that I am continually experiencing gratitude for those who allow me to share my gifts and who often remind me of how they appreciate my being in their lives. Teaching others allows me not only to share my knowledge and experience, but also allows me to learn from those I teach; not one group experience goes by where my participants have not taught me something that I needed to learn. I remember one workshop where a participant was a woman of such joy and generosity that I was convinced she was an angel! In spite of people teasing her about her optimism and enthusiasm, she continued to speak about her love of working with people and her joy for life. As I watched her, I realized that she reflected the love of life I often experienced, but did not always share with others. It's sometimes easier for me to voice my disappointments rather than my rewards. She taught me how sharing one's love for life and for others was a gift of immeasurable value.

In community, others provide us with situations that help us examine, refine and clarify who we are, what we have to offer, and how we can fulfill our purpose. They remind us that we are needed and appreciated, and that we have unique gifts that we can share. By bestowing our gifts and manifesting the blessings that emerge when others benefit from them, our lives and those of others are enriched.

Everyday Life

We also have the opportunity to use our lessons from religious practice and community in our every day lives. Since I am learning to be more compassionate, more forgiving, more curious, more present, in my religious community, I want to practice those same lessons in all my relationships. A rich lesson I have learned is how to listen to people I interview for team building workshops I facilitate. The interviewees are sometimes angry and frightened, make emotional judgments about others and are sometimes unwilling to take responsibility for their contributions to the difficulties. In listening to people, it was easy in the past for me to yield to my own incessant mental dialogue: "I can't believe they're saying that . . . how could that person do such a thing . . . don't they see their own roles in these events . . ." as I indulged in my own egotistical and judgmental conclusions about their attitudes and behaviors. As I have become more attuned to the spiritual implications of the art of listening, I have become more and more present; I recognize people's pain and frustration and fear. I see patterns in the information that I'm receiving that reflect the issues of the team. I empathize with their emotions while maintaining non-attachment that allows me to study and understand the nature of their particular group. Although earlier I would sometimes dread the depth of despair and pain I might encounter, I now recognize that I dreaded recognizing how their pain could mirror the hurting places in my own life. I began to realize that rather than my being judgmental, we all benefited by my recognizing our relatedness as human beings who experience difficulties, and by developing my ability to discern the truth about their circumstances. I could then focus on the team, rather than on my own reactions.

What's Missing Without a Spiritual Practice?

You might be thinking at this point that if religious practice offers community, a framework for living my life, an environment of beauty, and the motivation to manifest my practice in every day life, why bother with a solitary spiritual practice? What you may be missing is an opportunity to go deeper. For some people, a religious practice without a personal spiritual practice has limitations in its resources to help us experience the deepest spiritual life. It 's like the difference between loving music and being a musician. For those of us who are music lovers, we may involve ourselves in music in many different ways: we may study the period in which the music was written, learn about the lives of the composers, understand the different forms of the music, and immerse ourselves in the music when we listen to it. There are those people, however, who pursue their love of music with an even deeper commitment: they become musicians. They not only make the effort to appreciate the context and beauties of the music as we music lovers do, but they *make* the music. The music, in one sense, is literally created by them. They have the tactile experience of touching the instrument, coaxing the instrument to shout or whisper, cry out with joy or sigh with sadness. They become one with the instrument; it becomes an extension of themselves. Whether we are music lovers or the music makers does not make one group better or worse than the other. But the music makers engage their bodies and souls in the music, physically and with their senses, in a way that we music lovers don't. We music lovers only need to ask ourselves: if we feel sufficiently fulfilled to understand, treasure, listen to, and love the music? Or are we called to engage the music even more deeply, by bringing it into being?

In developing your own spirituality, you need to ask yourself those same questions: to what degree do you want to invite Spirit to be the center of your life, and how deeply do you wish to experience the intimacy with the Infinite? Do you feel fulfilled by pursuing a religious practice? Or are you called to go deeper? Pursuing a religious and spiritual practice is a profoundly rewarding and difficult journey. If you want to fully engage Spirit in a way that it forms, colors, and surrounds your life, you will want to take the next step from living a religious practice to pursuing a spiritual practice, too. You will want to know what it means to make the Infinite One the essence of your life.

Earlier in this book I defined spiritual practices as those activities which guide and assist people in making a more intimate connection with the Divine or universal; in Chapter 3, I'll talk about the specific reasons for pursuing a spiritual practice, but here are some of the key reasons a spiritual practice combined with a religious practice can deepen your personal spirituality.

The Rules

Rules and religious laws provide guidelines for living our lives, and we would live in chaos without them, for many of us apply those laws to our day-to-day actions, behaviors and decisions. When our religious practice focuses primarily on strictly "following the rules," however, it leaves little room for discernment, compassion, and, at times, doing the right thing in spite of the rules. A spiritual practice can develop our capacity to understand the paradox of honoring the rules while we explore the very depths of what it means, for example, to be compassionate. I heard a man on a radio talk show recently explain how a boy had tried to steal his car's tires, and instead of having the boy taken to juvenile hall, he brought him into his family, raised him, sent him to college and the boy is now leading a successful life. It would not have been wrong for the man to send the boy to juvenile hall; instead, he took a more compassionate route.

Van Pewthers shares these thoughts about the rules:

> The rules are simply there to give us the boundaries of what is beneficial to us. One of the things I've said is that the natural mind, that is the mind that has not been transformed by God, sees the Ten Commandments as the ten "don'ts": don't do this, don't do this, don't do this. But once you get the heart of the word, you take a look at what God's saying. It's not so much that the breaking of these rules are bad in and of themselves, but if I do these things, they break relationship; they take me on a path that takes me away from ultimately what is going to bring the greatest good, and that is being in relationship with God, being like God, being more like Him than I am right now. Without the devotional it's simply rule following.

If we follow a religious practice by the book, we may be limiting the self-exploration that allows us to make wiser, spiritual choices and act not only from our heads, but from our hearts, too.

The Meaning of Ritual

Many people approach ritual from an orthodox or established perspective. It's valuable to know the tradition of the ritual, and how to perform it with its intricacies and fine points, whether it is lighting Sabbath candles, reciting a prayer, or receiving the Eucharist. The dilemma that we can find ourselves in is that we can become obsessed with the "rightness" of the ritual, and we lose sight of the sacredness and devotional part of the ritual. We perform only out of fear of making a mistake or desire to make a good impression, rather than with reverence, out of obligation to perform the act rather than devotion, thoughtlessly rather than mindfully. Our focus narrows to doing the ritual precisely or correctly, rather than with love and commitment to that which is beyond our ability to comprehend or understand.

Another difficulty we encounter is falling into the practice of doing the ritual indifferently and without devotion or intent. Over time, it becomes boring: when lighting candles, we think of making dinner; when bowing, we wonder what the traffic will be like on the way home. Where religious practice teaches us the meaning of the ritual, spiritual practice nurtures our ability to practice ritual in a way that connects us with the richness and vastness of the Infinite. We can learn the skillful means for helping us to be present in the moment, such as remembering that each ritual connects us to our history or a particular story; reminds us that the candle is not separate from the divine light; and that when we bow to the Buddha, we honor all those who came before us, and every living being. These spiritual tools help us remember not only the symbolism of the ritual, but also remind us to practice the ritual as if we were dancing with the Divine.

Trapped in the Physical World

The Rev. Margie Clark, minister of the Church of Religious Science in Seal Beach, California says, "There is a danger with some religious practices. I've known people in our movement for a long time; they know everything, can quote from all kinds of sources, and it's astounding to me how much knowledge they have, but it hasn't penetrated them; it hasn't gone from the head to the heart, it hasn't become a part of them. Sometimes I think we study and read as a replacement for working on ourselves, so I see people who have built up a big shell of knowledge." And their shells prevent them from deeply understanding themselves and from relating intimately to both the human and the Divine. I greatly respect the importance of knowledge, which is an invaluable tool for learning how to act in the world, but it may also fall short of teaching us how to "be" in the world from a spiritual perspective.

Those who rely only on religious practice may find themselves being "Sabbath Sojourners," but not relating spirit to their everyday lives. They may sequester spirit into a 24-hour period and not make the transition to integrating spirit into their relationships and activities with family, friends, co-workers, and others with whom they interact daily. They become trapped by the demands of daily life, and don't have the resources to see the connection between religious beliefs, doctrine and laws, and how they can live their lives from moment to moment. A spiritual practice helps cultivate our potential for expansiveness, to bridge the gap between formal religious practice and the very nature of our lives.

Relationship with the Divine

Many religious practices focus on the Infinite being outside of ourselves, remote, obscure, and unreachable. You may see God as a "someone" of a particular gender whom you ask for things when you are desperate, hurt, frustrated or disappointed, and that "someone" gives you something back, if you are deserving. Once you take the path of a spiritual practice, however, paradox blasts apart every effort to nail down your perceptions and expectations of God. The Divine is both remote and present, subtle and apparent, outside and inside you, transcendent and available. You are created in the image of the Divine, but God has no image that you can adequately describe. Your desire to describe the Divine in human terms evolves into the aspiration to know that which cannot be defined. By maturing in your spiritual practice and relating it to your religious practice, you allow yourself to experience connectedness with that which is impossible to comprehend.

Rabbi Wayne Dosick, who leads the congregation Elijah's Minyan in San Diego, California says this about religious community and what's missing without the spiritual:

There's great value in community, and certainly we can do *mitzvahs* (good deeds) better in community, and certainly we can save Soviet Jewry and support the state of Israel and do all those kinds of things. So there are very good things about community, but at a certain point the community goes home, and the door closes, in Jewish terms, shiva (period of mourning following the death of a loved one) is over, and then the only thing that will make Judaism worthwhile for you and me is our own relationship with God, because all the rest isn't enough. And all the rest without God is empty and hollow. So there has to be this combination, this awareness, and this way to create this personal relationship with God.

Transformation

Father John McAndrew explains what's missing from our lives without a spiritual practice:

> What happens is that the story hasn't engaged your life. It's still somebody else's story. So in the Christian tradition you hear the story about Jesus, but it's 2,000 years ago, and he was a great man, but I can't do that. Whereas practitioners or spiritual persons, through spiritual discipline or their own life experiences, have encountered the story in a way that it took flesh for them. The Christian tradition uses the expression of Jesus, "the word became flesh," and that's what I think happens when people encounter that story, that word, and it suddenly begins to make sense in their experience. For Christianity, the defining story is the death and resurrection of Jesus Christ. That's a nice story, until a person goes through an experience that so shatters them that they have no way to put it together. Alcoholics Anonymous offers a way to do that, and traditional Christianity offers the same way. You die, so that something new, something different, can rise.

Religious practice can change your life, but for some, there will be limitations to the degree they will change within the confines of their faith. That degree of change may be more than sufficient for their lives to be enriched and fulfilled. But for others, the longing to be intimate with, and to experience the One in the deepest, most profound way, can only be achieved by plunging into the depths of their soul space, embracing joy and risking darkness, to know what it means to extinguish the separation between themselves and the Divine. And when they do this, their lives irreversibly change.

In the next chapter, we will explore in more depth the reasons for pursuing a spiritual practice. It is like diving to the depths of the deepest ocean, where the mysteries of life await us. When we learn to blend religious practice, which gives us community, framework and comfort, with a spiritual practice, which allows us to plumb the depths of the symbols and relationships which religious practice celebrates, we experience the greatest meaning and rewards of living the spiritual life.

CHAPTER THREE

Why Pursue
A Spiritual Practice?

Think of yourself as Ayin (nothingness) and forget yourself totally. Then you can transcend time, rising to the world of thought, where all is equal: life and death, ocean and dry land. Such is not the case if you are attached to the material nature of this world. If you think of yourself as something, then God cannot clothe himself in you, for God is infinite. No vessel can contain God, unless you think of yourself as Ayin.
~ DANIEL MOTT, *The Essential Kabbalah*

---

*I*t's evening; winter darkness hovers outside my sitting room. *I reach over and light a candle, then pick up the case of my* rakasu, *a bib-like garment made of dark fabric, representing the rice fields of Asia and the robes of Buddhist monks. I take the rakasu from its case, place it upon my head, and silently recite the Verse of the Kesa: "Vast is the robe of liberation, a formless field of benefaction, I wear the Tathagata's teaching, saving all sentient beings." The words touch me in different ways at different times, but this time they say, we all suffer at times in our lives, and the potential for liberating ourselves from our suffering can take life-times of effort and a single moment of surrender; we are released* *from delusion in those moments of freedom; and in wearing the rakasu, I celebrate the teachings of a lineage handed down over centuries, from teacher to student. As I receive those teachings and learn to live my life without grasping and without fear, I help others see the nature of their own suffering by holding up the mirror of their lives and working with them in compassionate ways. I put on my rakasu, bow to my pillow, bow to centuries of tradition, and sit on my zafu. For 30 minutes I am simply "being," opening up to each moment as it unfolds.*

I never tire of the moments just before I do sitting meditation or zazen. Even though I sit alone most evenings, I connect to a tradition that takes me beyond the everyday aggravations, frustrations, and challenges. Sitting trains me, and reminds me, that beyond my own limitations, narrow-mindedness and pettiness, my life is perfection, with nothing missing. I share with people all over the world a practice of Zen Buddhism that is meant to help us clarify our lives, deepen our relationship to our universe and appreciate each revealed moment.

Why Follow a Spiritual Practice?

Spiritual practices give us the opportunity to expand and perceive our lives on many levels; they are the practices that we often pursue in solitary, which allow us to experience a more intimate connection with the Divine or universal. When we are caught up in the mundane, dragged down by boredom, or disappointed with the experiences of our lives, a spiritual practice provides us with peace, understanding, gratitude, solace, and connection not only with the material world around us, but with the ineffable. In this chapter, you will learn about the precious quality of "being" versus "doing"; the beauty of communing with the Divine or connecting with the universal energy; the benefits of understanding the nature and interconnectedness of body and mind; the emergence and continual presence of gratitude in our lives; the restorative nature of practice; and replenishing your yearning soul space. You will also learn what is missing if you have only a spiritual practice without a religious practice.

The spiritual journey is one of mystery and profundity, of the simple and the sacred, and takes you both higher and deeper in your own spiritual life. Spiritual practice is the map that will guide you through the mountains and the valleys of the soul's journey—from the depths of despair to the exaltation of the profound. It is not always an easy path, or a pleasant path, but for many, it is the most rewarding and fulfilling, and the surest path to the Infinite One.

Rejoice in "Being"

In the summer of 1990, my husband and I moved back to California after a 13-year absence. It was culture shock for me on many levels, and I returned with ambivalence. I had left many dear friends in Colorado; I was going to start over my consulting practice "from scratch"; I had maintained few friends in California; I had a tenuous relationship with my sister who still lived here; and we came into a housing market that was greatly inflated compared to Colorado. Aside from trying to cope with the grief of leaving friends, the difficulty of making new friends, and searching for office space, I felt groundless, rootless and adrift. The most difficult adjustment was trying to keep pace with the California lifestyle: lots of freeway driving, lots of recreation to take advantage of, and lots of opportunity to fill my life with busyness. Keeping busy served as a temporary antidote to my loneliness, but instead of feeling fulfilled, I felt more and more frantic with the pace I had set and was finding impossible to keep up. It was shortly after the realization that my life was nearly out of control that I discovered Zen. The contrast between my busy day-to-day life and the simplicity of sitting on the pillow was so extreme, that I could not imagine sitting still for ten minutes, let alone for the hours that I eventually spent in intensive retreats. In spite of the seeming impossibility of sitting still, I was drawn to the opportunity to simply *be still*; to be present; to be receptive; to be here, now.

The more I sat zazen, the more I realized how I had unconsciously created my frenetic life of appointments and deadlines and incessant activity. I was able to witness the choices I was making, and realized I could choose to live differently. And I did. I cut back the pace, took time to reflect, and amazingly found that I was more productive, not less, and enjoying myself much more. More importantly was the subtle experience of simply "being."

When we take time to "be" in our lives, we begin to truly open to our lives as they reveal themselves. We see our lives more clearly; instead of being trapped by our choices, we begin to see that we have many more choices for living our lives in more meaningful ways. We also begin to appreciate stillness, how it opens up possibilities for relating to Spirit, and filling our soul space. If life has become constricted, it begins to expand. If we have bound ourselves up, our ties begin to loosen and fall away. Instead of being captivated or held captive by the demands we put on ourselves, we begin to realize how we have entrapped ourselves; we may stay where we are, but we will realize that seeing our lives as a trap is a matter of choice, and that we can choose to see our lives from more expansive and joyful perspectives.

Many people keep busy so that they never have to face the emptiness in their lives. By keeping busy, we never have time to reflect on our spiritual isolation, our loneliness, our desolation. Boredom becomes the enemy; we will do just about anything to keep from being bored, even when the effort increases our stress and anxiety. When we develop a spiritual practice that allows us to simply "be," we begin to understand the nature of boredom. Rather than judging it, we can study it with curiosity. When we are bored, we can, without discrimination, realize that it is simply another fleeting state of mind; that in one instant it can transform into wonder or joy.

When we make the time to simply "be" in our lives, we open ourselves to the potential of healing. Van Pewthers describes God's healing in this way:

> There's a dynamic where all of us in our growing up have gone through things that have hurt us. We've had parents who were less than they should have been or who were violent, angry or hurtful. For me to allow God to go into those areas, to bring healing to those areas, I have to have that sense of His presence and His courage that He gives me, to know that it's okay to revisit those areas and to allow His hand of healing to come in. Otherwise, because of the pain of those experiences, I'm not going to go there. In the Christian faith, even before we knew Him, Christ came and died for us; the implication is, God loved me

even when I wasn't lovable, even when I wasn't looking for Him, so if He loved me enough to do that, in those kinds of circumstances, that gives me the courage to believe that He'll love me when I bring the other broken parts of myself to Him.

Sometimes people think of healing as being sick and becoming well. Healing in our lives can happen in many different ways. We can invite healing, open to it, surrender to it, and although we may not be healed in traditional ways, we can be healed in our hearts and in our relationships with others. In my practice, I have experienced healing, particularly in those places where I felt hurt and desolate and alone. In my moments of "being," a sense of peace, harmony, and acceptance, for who I am and who I aspire to be, has filled my heart, and I have felt the mending of my soul space.

Perhaps most important though, when we learn to "be," we open ourselves up to a connection with God. We learn there is not any special thing to do or any special place to go, for to know the ultimate Spirit can occur in the simple act of surrender. Rabbi Steve Robbins says, "The meditative experience permits us to understand that we're never alone, unless we make ourselves alone. It provides us with a sense of autonomy, in that we know our place in the world, and that place is within us; it's not outside of us that we have to go find it." In stillness, we can open to the experience of each moment, and in each moment we make ourselves available to the transcendent that is beyond our comprehension, yet resides within us. Each passing moment of silence honors the Divine, as our senses interconnect us with It: in the warmth of the room, with the absence of sound, the smell of incense, the feel of the meditation pillow, we invite the Presence that can quiet our minds and open our hearts.

Communing with the Divine and Universal

When you are in a place of "being," you open yourself to the potential of relating intimately to the Divine. In the absence of the stress and distractions of every day life, you provide the time and space for recognizing and receiving the pervasive presence of God. For some, communing with the Divine can happen in other active ways as well, such as writing, art work, and singing. The key is to identify those practices that help you connect with the Other, that extinguish the separation you experience between you and the infinite. There are five key practices that I follow that help me to build bridges between God and me and between me and the universe: prayer, meditation, singing/chanting, journaling and ritual.

Prayer

I find great comfort in traditional Jewish prayer. When I pray to God, I am not just honoring my belief in that Presence beyond description and comprehension, but I remind myself that I can trust in that Presence and find solace in Its existence.

One focus of my personal evening prayers is on forgiveness, because inevitably I have acted in ways that have been detrimental to others and I desire forgiveness, or others have acted in ways that have disappointed or hurt me, and I have the opportunity to forgive them. Forgiveness is difficult for many of us, because it is so much easier to be angry with others, to be self-righteous about our disappointments in others or remorseful about our own failings. But when we don't forgive, we create barriers not only between ourselves and others, but between ourselves and the Divine. There is little room or energy for love, gratitude and compassion, and for connecting with God, when we are pre-occupied with our anger, hurt, disillusionment or fear.

My evening prayers are offerings that remind me that to forgive is to honor the struggles I share with others and repent the errors I have made; that when I honor and repent, I plant the seeds for experiencing my relatedness to God; that when I experience my relatedness to God, I am moved to love God with all my heart, soul and might, and that through my love of God I am compelled to practice and share my God-spirit; and with the fulfillment of having shared with and served others, I go to sleep at night expressing my gratitude for life and praying for another day to celebrate Spirit once more.

This cycle of communion and practice is like an upward spiral, because as I feel more connected to God, I am motivated to help others, and as I help others, I experience movingly and devotedly my relatedness to God. The spiral is not always positive and enjoyable, however; I sometimes experience moments of resentment for the demands of life and the expectations of others; I reflect on those times when God seems so remote that I grieve my inability to truly surrender to or experience the unknown. But if I see my spiritual path as whole and complete, whether I am perplexed or satisfied, frustrated or fulfilled, reluctant or enthusiastic, I remember that God is always present and the universe is perpetually expanding, whether or not I am fully or always aware of it. Linda Klassen, a Protestant and counselor in a missionary organization, says, "The greatest gift is the voice of God, finding that He really does want to speak to us. And He will find a way, when we're quiet enough to listen."

I am flying in a commercial jet, window seat, my head resting against the window, the sun touching my face through scattered clouds. I am thinking about my mother-in-law who is recovering from a broken hip from a fall, and suffers from the pain of arthritis—and fear. She has given up her freedom; she has stubbornly seized immobility as a preventative strategy to avoid pain and the risk of another fall. I ping-pong back and forth between compassion for her and frustration, understanding how frightened she must be, and disappointed that she doesn't stretch herself beyond her fear, choosing isolation and loneliness instead. I say a prayer, wishing for the experience of true compassion for her beyond my intellectually trying to comprehend her condition.

When I return home, I call my doctor who has left a message about some tests I completed a couple of weeks before. I'm surprised that she has called, since the only test results I haven't received are for bone density. And since I am following several regimens to prevent density problems, including proper diet, hormone therapy and exercise, I can't imagine why the doctor and I need to talk.

I return the doctor's call and after exchanging greetings, the doctor explains that the bone density in my wrist and spine are fine, but my hip bone density is below acceptable ranges, and I will need to take a prescription medication for bone loss. I am stunned. This couldn't be happening. The bone density test was

not even the doctor's idea; it was mine, a routine precaution. Af-
ter we decide on a medication, I mumble my good-byes and go
downstairs to sit in my favorite chair. I am furious! This is impos-
sible! As I rage, I ask myself what is underneath my anger. As I
meditate on this question, I recognize pulsating fear. "Hello, fear."
And suddenly I experience the thought, this is exactly how your
mother-in-law feels. My eyes fly open, and I begin to laugh and
cry at the same time. I am grateful I am alone in the house, for I
call out, that didn't take long! And then I moan, okay, I get it. So
this is how she feels. I sit for several moments to experience her/
our fear, and to acknowledge my genuine compassion for her, for
both of us.

When we pray, we open ourselves to the answers to difficult questions; we become receptive and available to that which is true, but at
times, seems unavailable. The lessons we learn, the self-knowledge we
acquire, the wisdom we attain may not always be easy or comfortable
for us. But they are all catalysts to deepening our relationship with
the Divine, and to recognizing the Divine voice in all of us.

Meditation

Meditation, or zazen in my Buddhist practice, is another way that I
commune with the universe. In the simple act of zazen, I make myself
available to each passing moment. The Rev. Margie Clark says about
meditation within her Christian practice: "We do meditation to open
us up to all kinds of realities that we don't experience or that we don't
even believe are possible. We do meditation for two reasons: one is to
know God, and one is to train our minds so we can. It's training that
allows us to know all of life more fully." For me, making myself available to each emerging moment of my life gives me many moments of
peace and fulfillment. When I have the ability to be attentive and aware,
I marvel at the wonder of my life opening with the passing of time, as
if I were watching a rose blooming, each delicate petal stretching out
to touch the sun's silken rays. When I meditate, I create a quiet environment that invites me to be fully present and available to each

unique moment. Nicolee Jikyo Miller-McMahon, Sensei shared these thoughts about zazen: "This is how I look at spiritual practice in everyday life. If you drew a circle, for example, and a hub in the middle, in the middle of the hub would be zazen. Coming out of that hub would be all these spokes like a roulette wheel, and zazen would be that which creates the stability to hold the space for everything. So when you're a priest, you're a priest, and when you're a mother, you're a mother, and when you're a wife, you're a wife; you just give completely to whatever you're doing. I find that the nurturing, the being spiritually fed, comes out of zazen."

Singing and Chanting

Another practice that makes me more available to the Divine is the singing of Jewish chants; I practice these on the Sabbath. Saturday is my time to sing to God. On Saturday mornings, I meditate, and then I progress through a series of chants provided to me by Metivta in Los Angeles. One of my favorite chants reads in Hebrew, *El Melech Ne-ehman; Shechinah malka ne-eh-ma-na.*

In English it translates, "God, trustworthy King; Divine Presence, trustworthy Queen." The tune is a plaintive one, and I feel my heart reaching backwards in time to the men and women of my Jewish roots. It encourages me to trust in God the King, in God the Shekinah, the exalted masculine and feminine aspects of the Divine. I repeat the chant over and over again, beginning very softly until it is a plaintive appeal to that part of me that is afraid to fully trust the Divine, to fully surrender to Its splendor and power, to Its nurturing and receptive presence.

Other chants remind me of God's healing, of my gratitude for being alive, of God's love and guidance, sovereignty, unity and holiness. After a few minutes of repeating a chant, moving from whisper, to crescendo, to whisper again, I then meditate on the theme of the chant. By putting chanting and meditation together, I experience a focused and emotional quality, a joy and ebullience different from simply sitting in silence. It is a blissful, enlivening and emotional experience that lifts my heart and gratifies my spirit, and is the highlight of my Sabbath observation and practice.

Journaling

Journaling provides me with answers, with consolation and clarity. When I journal, I don't just write down my thoughts (unless I can't think of a question to ask). Instead, I seek Divine wisdom to doubts, questions, concerns that I face day-to-day. We could argue whether God really answers me or I answer myself. I only know that I see my life from a different perspective after I ask a question, and am answered. Here is my journal entry of 2/17/99:

> How do I reconcile wanting to be glued to God [a Jewish concept] with non-attachment [a Zen Buddhist concept]?
>
> It is a paradox—one more opportunity not to reconcile, but to live with the reality of two apparently conflicting truths. In wanting your life to be entwined with Mine, you seek relationship and intimacy with that which is Other, and yet is part of you, that which is Divine yet of human form, that which is incomprehensible and yet full of wisdom. It makes no sense and yet it is desirable and attainable from your standpoint and from Mine. The key of non-attachment is not in the aspiration but in the process. It is seeking My love with no expectations of how, when or why it will be revealed or experienced. It is abiding with Me even when you experience Me as distant. It is thinking of Me, loving Me, even when you are hesitant to know My love in return. It is letting go again and again and again of any demand or hope of how I will love you, show you wisdom, provide you with strength, fill you with compassion. It is praying with Me for My sake, for your sake, for the world's sake, without expectation of how I will be revealed to you. So there is a conflict and there is not. Seek Me, know Me, love Me and do all of these with a moment's grace and with the joy of knowing that I am always here, and there is no One to seek and no place to go. For I am yours and you are Mine. Always.

I find great comfort in these words, because I have a little voice in my head that sometimes tells me that I'm not deserving, that it's all a fluke, and that I can never intimately experience God's presence. When I challenge that voice with the Divine voice within me, the voice that is in all of us if we are open to hearing it, I am rewarded with a reassurance and distinctness that silences my insecurities and hesitancy.

Whether God speaks to me, or I am simply profoundly moved by being in relationship with God does not matter to me. I simply feel blessed to be touched by the wisdom of Spirit.

Ritual

The last practice that has added richness to my spiritual practice is the practice of ritual. Although I follow many rituals in both Zen and Jewish communities, an individual spiritual practice that I have grown to love and appreciate is the lighting of the Sabbath candles to commemorate the beginning of the Sabbath, or Shabbas. Rabbi Wayne Dosick has taken this ancient ritual and reframed it in a way that not only allows me to honor an ancient tradition, but also allows me to touch the Divine:

> Shabbas is the remembrance of the moment of creation, so what's the first thing God did when he created? Let there be light, so we who are creating the illusion of God, imitating God, we create light. What we're doing is imitating that moment of creation. So if you stare into the candles for 30 or 60 seconds, they're not just candles: if you stare into the candles, it is possible that this week, or if it doesn't work this week, maybe next week or the week after, you will get in touch with that primordial moment of creation, and if you get in touch with that primordial moment of creation, you get in touch with the Creator. So it's a way in to God.

Another reason I practice ritual is that it gives me another opportunity to be fully attentive to the immediacy of my life and what it offers. At times in the Zen community I have the responsibility for the service position of doan, which is the person who rings most of the bells to cue everyone for each step of service; bells tell people when to bow, when to stand, when to sit; they announce the beginning and end of a series of bows; they remind people when a chant will begin and when it is about to end. I love to ring the bells, because it is a time to be fully engrossed in ceremony and spirit, to be fully awake to each step of the service, to be a guide and a musician at the same time. Each sound of a bell, whether a deep-throated call or melodious voice links me to hundreds of years of tradition and to my fellow practitioners in the present. At those times I am moving with the rhythm of ages, with sound and spirit, riding the stream of ancient wisdoms and contemporary quests. And my heart sings in harmony with the voices of bells.

Mind and Body Connection

It is a Sunday night and I'm hopeful that I will have a "quiet" 30-minute sitting period. I begin with three deep breaths, complete a scan of my body to try to bring my mind into connection with my body, and settle in. This is not going to be one of those quiet nights. My mind jumps from one thought to another like an excited puppy. Every time I lure it back, labeling the thought and sensing it in my body, my mind bounds back to the last thought, yipping and jumping in undisguised excitement. The puppy in me grabs hold of that juicy thought, braces its legs with tail in the air, and shakes its head from side to side, growling with delight. I finally tire of the exercise of turning thought into story, and remember what I came here for, and I take a deep breath. The puppy/thought circles on my sitting pillow and settles in. I note how the thought/story feels in my body. As each thought emerges, I watch it tugging at my mind, note its presence, and return to my breath.

There is much scientific evidence that speaks to the mind/body connection, that our thoughts and feelings directly affect the health and wellbeing of our bodies. Yet most of us treat our minds and bodies as if they were separate entities. For example, some of us worship our bodies: we exercise and diet incessantly, or have cosmetic surgeries, trying to manufacture the perfect body; others of us have a total disregard for our bodies, abusing ourselves by overeating or drinking in excess or smoking. Our motivations in either case, whether we are obsessed with the appearance of the body or oblivious to its wellbeing, are driven by the thoughts and feelings that we have. Whether we crave perfection or satiation, whether we make our bodies a monument to the artificial or a distorted testimony of excess, we have forgotten who we are: God's creation, God's temple. As long as we *think* that these approaches to life are good and right, we miss the point: we experience, exemplify and demonstrate universal love and kindness by *remembering* that we separate ourselves from others, from our universe, from the Divine when we fixate on the superficial and indulgent. It's not necessarily wrong or bad to care what we look like, or at times to disregard our bodies; but when we make our appearance the *focus* of our lives, or make the *focus* of our lives ingesting whatever satiates us, we render profane that which has been given to us: our human minds/bodies, which allow us to honor the sacred as no other living creature can.

Obsessions with the body or with the satisfaction of our appetites often seem out of our control. We may feel victimized by that which we desire, unable to turn away from that which lures us into more and more of the same self-centered thoughts and behaviors. When we finally realize that something is amiss, and *we really want to do something about it*, we can turn to spiritual practice to understand how the mind works, appreciate the nature of our lives, and how we actually have other choices about how we can live a life of Spirit. We begin to understand the complex interrelationship between the body and the mind.

We get into trouble when we think that our bodies and minds are separate entities, when in fact they are inextricably interconnected. We live in our minds, are slaves to our thoughts and feelings, and neglect the container that allows us to function in the material world. Through spiritual practice, we have the opportunity to realize fundamentally and intuitively that our minds and bodies are truly one entity, that they are interwoven and not separate. We begin to realize that our actions are driven by our feelings, that our feelings are manifest in our thoughts, and we begin to witness the complexity of our lives. Through stillness, we have the opportunity to reconcile the barriers we have created between our bodies and our minds, between our minds and our souls.

Through a meditative practice, we can observe the very nature of thought. As we try to sit quietly with a mantra or meditating on an object or following our breath, we become a witness to the operations of our minds, the thought process; we finally notice how our thoughts are incessant, persistent and unending. Instead of indulging in and investing in our thoughts, we can dispassionately observe how our minds operate, the kinds of thoughts we have. We can notice the very nature of our thinking, how our thoughts are self-indulgent, transient and continuous. Instead of seeing our thoughts as the very center of our lives, we realize they are often elusive, petty, redundant and even amusing. Ironically, though, instead of judging and criticizing ourselves, we can simply recognize the very human nature of thought, how it creates barriers not only between ourselves and others, between our minds and our bodies, but also between ourselves and God. The more we meditate, the more we realize that we have more choices about the time and energy we want to devote to thinking; we can choose to watch the nature of our thoughts, but not become obsessed with them; we can choose instead to open to the present moment, to its unique and special quality, and to its unfixed nature.

As we open to the very nature of thought, we can begin to focus on its relationship to our bodies, and recognize that our bodies are never separate from who we are or what we think. Every thought has a quality to it: it may reflect a desire that we have; or it might reflect our anger about something; or it might reflect restlessness or boredom, or even the very doubts we may have about spiritual practice.

To bridge the gap between body and mind, we can begin to label our thoughts and notice how they manifest in our bodies: do we experience a pleasant sensation, an unpleasant sensation, or a neutral sensation? My sensei has given me this practice, and its effects on me have been profound. As I follow my breath during meditation, I find it easier and easier to observe the nature of my mind; I notice a thought—"oh, I'd love to show them how to deal with their fear" in a workshop, and realize that I desire to help others understand fear; when I label the thought, I then notice its sensation in my body, which in this case is often pleasant, because even though the experience of fear itself is unpleasant, teaching others about the nature of fear gives me great satisfaction. Working with thoughts in this way may seem cumbersome at first; however, once you get the hang of it, labeling a thought and recognizing its sensation in the body only takes a moment. Joseph Goldstein and Jack Kornfield, in their book *Seeking the Heart of Wisdom: The Path of Insight Meditation*,[1] explain these practices in depth, and how working with them can help us lead happier lives.

Before I began to work with the nature of the body/mind connection, I experienced so much conflict, that there was little room for Spirit, and the little space that was available was filled with chaos. For me, understanding the nature of the body and mind and recognizing their interconnectedness has opened my heart. I've begun to understand how my body and mind are interconnected. When my mind is "unwell," my body suffers; when my body is unwell, my mind suffers. I am self-absorbed, unavailable and unable to relate to God and to those around me, until the moment when I recognize how I am allowing my body or mind to separate me from God; then I have the opportunity to shift my perspective and open to my life, as it is. When my mind is healthy, my body benefits, and when my body is healthy, my mind benefits; I sense and rejoice in God's presence and am motivated to help others. The more I am in tune with the connection of body and mind, the more I experience my life as congruent and whole. The more whole my life becomes, the more open I become to inviting in and welcoming Spirit into my life. Then body and mind become a receptacle for, a haven for Spirit, and I experience my life as more integrated and complete.

Gratitude

How much time do you spend thinking about disappointments, losses and frustrations? Do you think about the things you want to have, instead of appreciating the things you do have? Do you work long hours to acquire more material possessions? Do you complain about your boss, your job, your wife or husband, or your children? Do you wish you had more friends, better friends?

Many of us spend a lot of time seeing our lives from a perspective of loss or incompleteness. We wish for life to be different, to have

---

1. Joseph Goldstein and Jack Kornfield. *Seeking the Heart of Wisdom: The Path of Insight Meditation*. Boston: Shambhala, 1987.

more—more fun, nicer cars, bigger homes, better bodies. Life becomes a reflection on what we lack and what we've lost; how we've been betrayed or cheated. And although we have moments when we know we *should* be grateful, we express gratitude grudgingly and resentfully.

When we pursue a spiritual practice, we begin to emerge from a perspective of neediness and scarcity to a life of fulfillment and gratitude. We see gifts everywhere—in the person who smiles at us, when a spouse says we are loved, when a student shares a creative insight.

I have found that I am frequently (and gladly!) overwhelmed with gratitude nearly every day of my life. This morning, as I sit at my computer, I am grateful for my good health; for the opportunity to be able to take a morning to write; for the pine trees outside my window, waving at me in the wind; for a husband only a few steps away whom I can give a kiss each time I get up to stretch; for the inspiration I experience when I reflect on living a life of Spirit. When I pursue a spiritual practice, my life transforms in a way that allows me to see the difficult circumstances of my life from a broader perspective, as temporary and insubstantial. Instead of obsessing on the negative, I begin to experience gratitude. I often have moments of intense peace and satisfaction, where I may simply pause and say, "thank you, God," or the equivalent in Hebrew, "Baruch HaShem." Sometimes my gratitude comes from the mundane, such as being hired for a noteworthy and challenging project; sometimes my gratitude comes from having my smile returned from the little girl next door; sometimes my gratitude comes from my husband sneaking up from behind and giving me a big hug. My life is full of blessings, and I've only begun to recognize the multitude of blessings, which are sometimes the gifts of God's grace, as my spiritual practice has matured over time. Words of thanks seem to come forth naturally, from moments of awareness, when I emerge from my self-consciousness and self-absorption and realize how magical and glorious life is.

I've also found that gratitude can be expressed in many other ways, such as serving others in my Zen community, through my work, with my husband and friends. By serving them, I provide them the chance to know the meaning of gratitude, and in those moments they can transcend their day-to-day grievances and experience for themselves the gift of appreciation. And of course, as they experience gratitude, I experience my own gratitude for being available and being able to help.

There doesn't seem to be a specific or particularly magical part of my practice that has allowed gratitude to show up in my life. Rather, it is the persistence and regularity of my practice that I believe has made the difference. It isn't even whether I meditate for 15 minutes or 30 minutes, or once or twice a day (although I believe there is a cumulative effect that can increase the magnitude of the grateful experience). I think it is making time to practice every day, devoting time to be present to the entirety of my life, that allows not only for my feelings about my trials to manifest, but creates the space for balancing those feelings with fulfillment and the beauty of pure joy.

Spiritual practice also creates the energy and space to repeatedly recognize that we can transcend those places where we get stuck and know the gifts that life has to offer. Gratitude emerges naturally, organically; it's as if we've planted precious seeds, watered and fertilized them, let them rest in the sunshine, and then simply watch them grow. But as they begin to grow, there is still effort to be made: we need to cover them if the weather gets too cold, pull the weeds that want to share their space, protect them from bugs and animals that may want to eat them as much as we do. The practice of growing the seeds never ends. We can see that effort as time consuming, tedious, and wasted, or we can see it from a perspective of gratitude, as we are nurtured, captivated and fulfilled. How we choose to see our spiritual practices, to see our lives, is truly up to us.

The Restorative Nature of Practice

Recently a potential client asked me about working with a group of people who were responsible for paving streets. They worked in a difficult environment, particularly in the summer when the heat could be unbearable. Some members of the group seemed to be unhappy a lot of the time, and tended to create dissension in the rest of the group. When I commented to management about the misfortune of these people leading lives of such unhappiness, I also added that I wondered if they realized how important their jobs were and how we all relied upon them—how would we be able to drive our cars safely if they were not available to regularly maintain the streets? I was told that these workers probably did not see their roles in that way, particularly in the stifling heat of summer.

All of us have probably experienced times in our lives when we questioned what we were doing. Whether you are a homemaker, a gas station attendant, a financial advisor, a teacher, or a politician, you have probably asked yourself, "Is this all there is to life? Is this what I want to be doing the rest of my life?" Some of us seem doomed to lead unhappy lives, no matter what we do; we are never satisfied, pleased or joyful. We see our lives as meaningless, worthless and are perpetually sad.

A spiritual practice can initiate a subtle transformation in those of us who lack meaning in our lives: it allows us to see our lives as full and complete, regardless of what we are doing. It helps us see the satisfactions within difficulty, the symmetry within disruption, the benefits within losses. When we lose this balanced perspective, we suffer from burn-out. Burn-out comes from the loss we experience when we realize that we can never attain our ideal for work: that we will never successfully train every student, never attain perfection, never please everyone. Intellectually we know these truths, but we fight them, we resist them and we grieve over losing our ideal; our lives seem to lose meaning and purpose.

When I invest time in a regular spiritual practice, my mind and heart encompass and accept all that my work has to offer including rewards and limitations. When I conduct a training program, not every participant will change his or her behaviors following the training—but I will have touched every person's life. I went through a period years ago when I began to wonder about the meaningfulness of my work—until I realized the absurdity of the questions I was asking: would every single participant have to learn and utilize my training for me to be successful and satisfied? Would 50% have to go along, or 30% or 10%? Then I realized that I had absolutely no control over what anyone else *chose to learn* or not. The only thing I could do in my training and facilitation was to do my very best on a given day, to be receptive and available, or as circumstances dictated, tough and direct. But if I brought my best self to the training, then I was fulfilling my purpose. As Swami Sarvadevananda of the Vedanta Society says, "One person can give peace to thousands."

One of the most beautiful aspects of Judaism is the role of the Jew: to heal or mend the world. That's what God asks of each Jew. God doesn't say we have to *make* other people change, or become better or smarter or wiser or more compassionate; God says that the role of the Jew is to make the effort to make the world a better place. God doesn't give us an instruction manual or measurements for the success of these actions, or tell us how much time we should spend, or the roles we should pursue to do it. I may help heal the world in my own way by making a sad clerk in a store laugh; or by giving a shy friend a hug; or by listening and being present to the frustrations of a client. My spiritual practice has helped me develop the abilities to do these things in ways I never thought I could. I am reminded that my mission in life is not to make other people's lives ideal, but to continue to grow in my own spiritual development so that I might simply be available to those who need me or want my help. Being available doesn't mean just showing up; it means showing up with a willing ear and an open heart. Even when I train people, I have often learned that they have as much to teach me as I have to teach them—or more. My spiritual practice has shown me that my desire to be the perfect healer is futile, and has allowed me to work at letting go of perfection, to be accessible to others, and pursue my own personal growth.

Some of my work can be very difficult; in team building workshops, people are often afraid and angry, blaming and resistant. In the past when I was busy with a number of projects, I would become exhausted, both physically and emotionally. Much of my energy was directed at trying to force others to change, or to be different, or to see the errors of their ways. Although many times I was rewarded and often touched at the efforts of the workshop participants, I was also frustrated and perplexed at the determination of others to continue to behave in counterproductive ways.

As I continued to pursue my spiritual practice, I began to see how I was exhausting myself. Although I knew intellectually that people would change only if they wanted to change, I kept thinking that I could somehow transform them in spite of their resistance to acting differently. My sensei gave me the spiritual practice of asking myself when I experienced this frustration, "What is it I'm wanting?" My answer would be "To get people to see how they are acting destructively and to get them to change!" The next step was asking myself, "What are the chances that the most resistant people will comply?" My honest answer was, "Slim to none, particularly when I'm pushing them." That's when I realized that a profound spiritual practice for me would be the practice of letting go, over and over and over again, of getting people to change.

At first I struggled with this effort of letting go, thinking I had to force myself to think differently. The more I practiced with letting go, however, I realized that in fact there was really nothing for me to "do." All I had to do was simply let go, open myself to the truth of the nature of change. Letting go of my expectations of others has not occurred overnight, and is still a work in progress; it will be, for me, a lifetime process, letting go over and over again to that which I cannot control or change. But my spiritual practice has also taught me that letting go is incredibly liberating; there is nothing to force to happen, there is nothing I can make happen. I simply need to be present, to speak the truth, to sometimes set limits and boundaries if needed, and to watch what develops. As I have matured in my ability to let go of the need to change others, and as I stop pushing, but instead have created space for them to contemplate how they relate to life, they are more likely to change on their own. Perhaps because their energy does not go into resisting me, they instead can allow their energy to rest and they open to other possibilities.

The enormous benefit of letting go is that my work has become more and more fulfilling and energy building for me, instead of draining and difficult. I have more stamina to help others and feel more energized in my work projects. The attitude that once exhausted and drained me spiritually, emotionally and physically is now replaced with a sense of enthusiasm, purpose and mission, and a clearer understanding of how I can enrich my own life and contribute to the welfare of others.

The Mystery of the Journey

Many of us preoccupy ourselves with the noise and demands of our lives, so that we don't have to hear the echoes of loneliness and recognize our consuming fear of the unknown. Although we may have an intellectual belief in God as a separate and distant entity, we have little intimate understanding and appreciation of God's love in our life. If God is always there, if we truly are not separate from the universe, how do we overcome our isolation and fear and invite God to be intimate with us? I suggest it is through spiritual practice.

While we spend time every day eating at least three meals, and probably working in some snacks, too, to nourish our bodies, we often starve our souls. Our soul space cries out for such attention, but we neglect it for activities that are frivolous or more acceptable. Who would argue that it's worthwhile to do laundry or clean the house? Who would debate that sitting in front of the television or reading a good novel can be relaxing and pleasurable? Who would deny that it's important to work hard to be a good performer in our jobs? We are willing to invest time in these conventional activities, and pretend that we have no time for anything else—including the most divine and esoteric parts of our lives.

We neglect our spiritual lives for the mundane and the profane, and we resist spiritual pursuits, because we don't know what we'll discover when we begin the journey. The irony is that we don't transform into something or someone completely different from who we are when we are in relationship with God; instead, we simply discover more truly who we really are, we recognize the very best parts of ourselves, that which is the perfection, that which is the Divine. The enrichment of filling our soul space cannot be matched with any material pursuit, which one way or another provides only temporary and fleeting satisfaction. When we begin to replenish our soul space, we may, on a given day, be less aware of God's presence; but at a time when we may least expect it, God fills our hearts and souls, and we are reminded of God's constant and pervasive love.

Spiritual Highs

Spiritual highs are like chocolate chip cookies. There's nothing like a chewy chocolate chipper, the rich chocolate and sugar coursing through my veins. I'd love to find a way to eat chocolate chip cookies for every meal and have them for dessert, too. But after a while, I know that, although the cookies would keep me from getting hungry, a steady diet of them would take their toll. I'd find that the sugar high was not enough; I'd probably put on weight; the constant sugar diet would make me lethargic and listless; the specialness of the cookie would turn to ordinariness, and I'd be looking somewhere else to get my "cookie high."

Although a spiritual high can be rewarding, it is also temporary. If we're not careful, we can make spiritual highs our goal and motivation for spiritual practice, and we begin craving them and having them become the focal point of our lives. Instead of filling our soul space with depth, relationship with spirit, and constancy, we only touch that yearning void with occasional spiritual stimulants that are transitory and impermanent. Rabbi Jonathan Omer-Man speaks about the limitations of pursuing a spiritual life only for the spiritual highs. "I know some people who have been thrown into despair by the fact that they've had a profound spiritual experience and realize they may never have that kind of experience again. In fact, I was working two years with someone who had the a series of experiences with the Divine; he had the most incredible experiences of getting up every day and seeing the world as infused with the Divine and love and laughter everywhere, and suddenly it wasn't there anymore. He went away in such great despair, because he realized he might never get there again."

There is nothing good or bad about these experiences; they are simply gifts. If we see them as the center of our spirituality, however, we miss realizing and appreciating the Divine in the simplest aspects of our every day lives. For most of us, every moment does not become one of wonder or awareness of the Divine; instead we have more and more moments when we recognize the Divine in our lives. Our spiritual practices help us make these connections in the most basic of circumstances, whether we awaken to morning silence, share a meal, listen to a friend, or wash the dishes.

Instead of abandoning a spiritual practice when we don't have a sufficient number of spiritual highs, we can use our experiences as a way to remind us that there *is* a sacred dimension to life worth experiencing, that there *is* a worthy path. The Reverend John "Jake" Jiyu Gage of the Three Treasures Zen Community speaks this way of spiritual experiences:

> If a person has not had a religious or spiritual practice before, and something gives the person this taste of the Divine, at that point he or she will be on the path continuing to seek the Divine, because the experience is so completely satisfying and completely full. It's like a moth to a flame; you're just pulled. After a while you realize there's nothing you can do and you just have to give in and go with the flow of the stream. If you ask how does the experience of the Divine change one's life, well, the Divine is already changing our lives; all we have to do is just let go. Life becomes worth living, becomes joyful and infinitely interesting and challenging, but challenging in a whole new way, in that I now want to share it with others.

Sister Jane DeLisle also talks about the need to come into relationship with God:

> God works through the circumstances of my life and changes my life. I've got to be willing to be open to that. It's that willingness to let go of the one thing that I've held on to most of my life that's given me protection, in order for God to be able to work through me. I've got to say that I surrender that protection to go deeper in relationship with myself, in relationship to God and in relationship to other people. As we open, we become more and more who God calls us to be. If you let yourself go there, you experience a spiraling deeper and deeper to where God dwells within."

Without a spiritual practice, our lives may be like a tightly folded bud that never fully blossoms and dies on the vine: it's experienced its life cycle as an emerging flower, but never completely opened to all its possibilities.

Not only do we experience more intimately our relationship with God, but we discover the Divine or universal in ourselves. Linda Klassen, counselor in a Protestant missionary organization says, "Spiritual practice is life-giving, that which enables us to grow, that which is most central in myself, that which is most essentially made in the image of God, that light of God from which our life springs." The Venerable Thich Chon Thanh of the Lien Hoa Temple in Garden Grove, California describes how we discover the vastness of our true nature, which could also be defined as our divine nature, or Buddha nature:

> When our mind is very clear, we see our Buddha nature. Tonight you might feel very, very tired, but tomorrow morning you get up, and if you slept very well, you feel better and your mind is clear. [The Venerable points to a mirror nearby.] If this mirror is covered with dust, we can hold up a finger and it will not reflect in the mirror, but if we clean the mirror and hold up a finger, it reflects beautifully as the mind does when it is clear. And if we clean up the mirror beautifully, the butterfly reflects in the mirror beautifully. Your Buddha nature looks like the mirror; worldly desire covers Buddha nature. If we clean up the worldly desires, we can understand everything and we become Buddha.

When we practice spiritually, not only do our minds become clearer, but our hearts begin to open, too. The barriers that we have built around our hearts start to fall apart, and although it can be unnerving to see how our lives begin to open to others, we begin to realize that the constraints that we have established have not allowed us to acknowledge the Divine. We can see ourselves as allowing the Divine in, or letting the Divine within us emerge, or both. Either way, we allow the All to permeate our lives, our perspectives and our hearts. And once we pursue this path, our lives will never be the same.

What's Missing Without a Religious Practice?

Following a regular spiritual practice is key to a deep spiritual life. There are limitations to pursuing only a spiritual practice without community, however — many of the benefits of religious community are covered in more detail in Chapter Two. I feel the limitations to developing a rich spiritual practice without religious community include (1) distorting the sense of self, (2) loss of grounding to tradition, (3) limitations to growth, and 4) missing your purpose.

Distorting the Sense of Self

When you have a regular spiritual practice, you will likely begin to feel better spiritually, emotionally, even physically. From this sense of well-being, you may eventually develop a different view of who you are. You may feel more centered, more grounded, more at peace. Events that have disturbed you in the past become less important; you may be less reactive to the unexpected, more understanding of differences and more forgiving of disappointments. Your worldview may become more inclusive and less judgmental. People who have aggravated or frustrated you in the past have less impact on you. You may find you relate to the world in a more loving and compassionate way. Simple things bring you joy and satisfaction; you notice the blueness of the sky, the scent of flowers, the bright green of the grass, your fondness for others. Life seems more vibrant and rewarding.

Eventually, though, when you practice alone, your ego can get in the way of your spiritual development. You may begin to see yourself as "more spiritual" than others, superior to those who live more mundane lives. In some cases, you may believe that your spiritual view is "better" than others, that others are misled and that you are following the most authentic path. What was once an open, receptive, tolerant and embracing view of the world can begin to rigidify and be exclusive.

At first glance, this description might seem excessive or exaggerated; you might not be able to imagine yourself "going off the deep end"; however, when you are in this isolated spiritual place, without any input or feedback about your attitudes and behaviors, there is no way objectively to realize where you are. It's as if you've begun to live in a fun house of distorted mirrors, and after a while, if that is all you see, the distorted images reflect your reality.

In community, you have the opportunity to get feedback when you get off track. Pastor Craig Lockwood of the Vineyard Christian Fellowship says, "A Christian community confronts us or gives us feedback, and keeps people going on the road to truth. Sometimes we lose our sense of reality in isolation; without community, there is no form that keeps us on the right track or helps us stay in the direction we should be going." Pastor Preston Price of the United Methodist Church explains the limitations of a spiritual practice without community in a similar way: "With just the individual experience, you're missing community. You are not subjecting what you hear to the judgment of others, so solitary prayer may go off the deep end, unless someone else says, 'Wait, I don't hear that from God.' So you're in danger of feeding yourself, almost cannibalizing on your own needs, desires, wants and dreams, and you can fool yourself into thinking you're hearing God, but you're hearing yourself. So the community offers a balance."

In pursuing only an individual spiritual practice, you miss the opportunity to share the joys of your experience. The Rev. Murray Finck says, "When things seem to be going well in our spiritual journey, at least it works this way for me, I want to be able to give that away to another person. I want them to experience that, too. It's too good for me to keep to myself. They don't have to do it my way; I just want them to know what is really uplifting and encouraging and strengthening for me."

In community, you are not only loved and supported because you share a spiritual pursuit with others; those in community also show their love for you by speaking the truth when you might not want to hear it. The community members can speak to you when you have taken a wrong turn, when you are misled by your delusions of practice, and when you are hurting yourself or others. When you are immersed in a spiritual journey, you may have difficulty recognizing when you have fallen off the path. The community can help you by lifting you up, brushing you off, embracing you with the love of friendship, and helping you get back on the path.

Loss of Grounding to Tradition

To a person of western culture, this loss, at first glance, may not seem very important. Most of us have been raised to believe in progress, modernization and innovation, and don't appreciate or may disdain that which is ancient, culturally obscure and without modern meaning. I'm not against that which is modern; I love my washing machine, car and airline travel as much as the next person; I celebrate our medical victories over smallpox and polio; I appreciate our 20th century efforts around peace and equality. I regret, however, that many people feel they must denigrate the past if they celebrate the present and future; there is a great loss in this belief.

Religious community often offers us many benefits and blessings. First, it provides us an opportunity to be connected to a history and tradition; it reminds us that although our current religious community may be contemporary or a modification of ancient beliefs, there were *people* who devoted their lives to codifying and communicating the systems in which we believe and which we practice. Nicolee Miller-McMahon, Sensei says, "Western culture lives in such a world of immediacy; but the relatedness to something that goes beyond immediate gratification and comes out of the past can be a spiritual practice. So if we are only taking care of our own needs and we don't feel our connection to tradition, I think we really miss something, and religion offers that: it reminds us that we are in a context of humanity flowing through a stream, and where that stream goes, we don't know, but we're all in it together."

Second, there were people who sacrificed, struggled with belief and devoted themselves to spirit—just like we do; they made mistakes, wrestled with faith, gave up the comforts of their homes, railed against the difficulties of practice—just like we do. So when we see ourselves as different from the tradition, we can remember that human beings, just like us, have always struggled with the same issues of human aspiration. And so we connect with the humanity of spirit.

Third, in some traditions we are exposed to cultural practices that challenge our beliefs and comfort zones about "modern practice." For example, in Judaism you are exposed to numerous cultures and histories, whether you build a *sukkah*, part of an ancient harvest ceremony, for the holiday of Sukkot, or dance with the Torah in the community for Simhat Torah. Or in Zen Buddhism, you may chant in Japanese or wear long robes and bow. We can see these communal religious practices as foreign (and therefore un-Western or offensive), or we can use them as an opportunity to learn about other cultures and our heritage, identify with practices that are hundreds of years old, and immerse ourselves in ancient traditions that allow us to relate to the timelessness of the universal.

So when we practice alone, whether we practice with prayer, meditation, chant or movement, we miss the sense of connectedness that comes with tradition and community. Although I sometimes sing Jewish chants alone, I have a totally different experience when I sing and chant with others. When my voice joins with the voices of others, we are relating to each other, celebrating with each other, praying with each other in a way that produces a richness, a merging of our spiritual quests. It is no longer I alone who am seeking God; instead, we are helping each other, with ancient and modern practices, to seek God together.

Limitations to Growth

Spiritual practice is about relationship. If we only have an individual spiritual practice and no community, we may be led into believing that the "relationship" is only about relating to the universal or to God. This belief is incomplete. A spiritual practice that allows us to relate to God also has to guide us and teach us about being in relationship *with others*. For if we don't take our practice into the world, allow ourselves to be influenced and moved by others who understand, identify with and support our spiritual journey, we limit the opportunity to test and strengthen our spiritual lives.

I concluded my interview with Van Pewthers and Craig Lockwood, pastors at that time with the Vineyard Christian Fellowship. It was my second interview with them, and we'd developed a rapport and appreciation of each other. As I packed up my notes and prepared to leave, Van asked me if I would mind if they both prayed for me before I left. I was surprised, then deeply moved by their offer. I smiled and responded, "Of course—I can use all the blessings I can get."

Having grown up in a Jewish tradition and more recently begun a Zen practice, I didn't know what to expect from Christian pastors. As I sat in my chair, hands resting in my lap, Van and Craig stood next to me, and Van explained that he hoped it was

okay if they touched me, which he explained meant simply plac-
ing a hand on my head or shoulder. I smiled and said "no prob-
lem," and waited for them to begin.

As they both recited blessings, spontaneously and from the
Bible, I found myself deeply moved. Here were two men, who knew
my spiritual practice was quite different from theirs in many ways,
and yet they wanted to wish me well on my journey. As Van placed
his hand on my head, and Craig rested his hand on my shoulder,
I felt our energies and devotion to that which is holy intermingle
and expand. Independently and concurrently, they prayed for me.
At times I closed my eyes, at moments overcome with their gener-
osity and at other times filled with gratitude. As I listened to what
they were saying, I was especially touched by the fact that they,
intentionally or not, were limiting their appeals to God, rather
than including Jesus Christ who, as the son of God in Christian
tradition, was not a part of my own personal practices. I breathed
in their good wishes and hopes, and breathed out my own bless-
ings to them in return. They both sensed when they had completed
their prayers, and after a moment of silence, I thanked them with
tears in my eyes for their kindness and support.

When we are in relationship with others in religious community, we have the opportunity to grow beyond the superficial and relate to others of like spiritual mind in much deeper ways. We are tested in our willingness and ability to make ourselves vulnerable, to open to each moment before us and to share our gifts with others. We can learn to express and offer love and compassion to others; we can hold the mirror up to others when they are off track, and risk rejection; we can listen to others when they are suffering, and simply be a sympathetic ear without having to fix or repair their lives. We can simply learn to expand our awareness, explore the depths of our feelings for others and be available when we are needed. We can be willing to open ourselves to the hurt and devastation of others, and simply make our gift to them the willingness to be present without making their distress any more, or any less.

These moments offer emotional challenges that many of us simply cannot experience when we practice alone. A personal spiritual practice can be a place of refuge, but it can also be a place to hide. By being in community, we are forced out of our seclusion to practice in the real world with people who respect and share our journey, and who need our comfort and support. Whether I am on the receiving end of someone's anger or joy, frustration or contentedness, directed at me or about someone else, I can realize that it is not just her anger or joy that I experience; that her expressions are the same as my anger and joy, my moments of ecstasy or desolation that she mirrors, that we are both creatures that experience deep feelings in our relationship with ourselves, to each other and to the world.

The paradox is that we begin to feel less vulnerable as we allow ourselves to become more vulnerable. We recognize that our fear is an illusion and not really a barrier to our relationships and to spiritual development, and more and more we allow ourselves to be more available, to demonstrate compassion, to express love. Even if we realize that to make ourselves emotionally vulnerable is at times frightening, we know that there are others in religious community who are also frightened and are also willing to take the risks of exposure and accessibility because of the potential benefits of spiritual growth—offered only in community.

Missing Your Purpose

In the material world, we express our goals in fairly predictable ways: we want to be successful, to be well thought-of, to be prosperous, to be happy. We tend to focus on the everyday frustrations of our life: the friend who is unavailable, the boss who overloads us with work, the child who gets into trouble, the freeway driver who cuts us off. For some, life is just something to get through with a minimum amount of trauma. We focus on ways to limit our exposure, on how to remain safe, on how to keep things steady and the same. The irony is that we have almost no control over any aspect of our lives. All our efforts to keep things under control and predictable are subject to the whims of happenstance, and yet we rail against those forces that we cannot manipulate and manage.

As my own spiritual practice has deepened, I continually remind myself that I have little control over anything. Sure, I can set my alarm in the morning to make sure I get up on time, but I have no control over whether the alarm will actually wake me, over whether I'll feel rested when I wake up, over whether I trip on the way to the bathroom and pull my back, over whether my hair is easy or difficult to style that morning, and on and on and on . . . No matter how much time I spend planning my day, there are endless numbers of circumstances which I cannot monitor or influence. When I first got a glimmer of this truth, I approached it intellectually. I said to myself, "I understand," but in my heart I was fooling myself.

As the reality of my life being in constant change and flux began to sink in, I began to think, "If my life is so out of control, what in the world am I doing here?" In that moment, I experienced a brief and sometimes elusive truth: My life means more than my every day plans and desires; I must be here for more than having a job, being a wife, cooking meals, writing an article. I found this truth enormously liberating, because it freed me up to explore whether I had a different, higher purpose for being here. Concurrent with these thoughts, I began to genuinely get in touch with the reality of this truth, as I regularly attended my Zen Center. Every Tuesday I could plan on being with like-minded people who supported my spiritual growth. As my spiritual friends, particularly my sensei, generously supported my journey, I felt enormous gratitude and love for them. In one respect, *we have to make the spiritual journey alone.* No one can do the hard work for us: no one can mend our hearts or show us God or fill our soul space. Yet at the same time, paradoxically, *we don't have to make this journey alone.* If we do, we miss the precious and joyous opportunities to be strengthened in our practice, to be supported, to share our gifts, and to identify with a past and future tradition that exists right here, right now.

CHAPTER FOUR

What Does it Mean to Have A Religious/Spiritual Path?

Communal and individual prayer belong together as two folded hands. Without community, individual prayer easily degenerates into egocentric and eccentric behavior, but without individual prayer, the prayer of the community quickly becomes a meaningless routine.
~ HENRI NOUWEN, *Reaching Out*

*I*t's Tuesday evening, 5:45 p.m. and I'm dashing out of the house and making my way to Three Treasures Zen Community in Vista for Tuesday night service and sitting. I know I'm cutting it close, because I want to change clothes when I get there, but I push the speed limit and hope the highway patrol is on dinner break.

As I arrive at Jake's house, which doubles as our Zen Center, I grab my bag stuffed with my sitting pillow, my rakasu (a bib-like piece worn by Buddhists), my robe and kimono. I kick off my shoes at the front door and share a perfunctory hello to whoever crosses my path, and make a dash for the bathroom, hoping that it's empty so I can change clothes. As I toss my street clothes into the bag, I take a few deep breaths, feeling my body and mind making the *transition from the daily world into the tranquility of the* zendo *(sitting room). Belting the kimono, fastening the robe and taking one last look to be sure I've not left anything on the bathroom floor, I throw open the door and head to the entry room just off the zendo, which was converted from a recreation room by Jake. The pool table doubles as a large altar, and I glance and smile at the fresh flowers which have Carolyn's touch, and at those who are quietly standing in anticipation of service beginning. I shove my bag into a corner and take another deep breath. As I turn, Jikyo Sensei looks at me with her usual look of delight to see me (which I know she shares with everyone, but has a way of making each one of us feel special with just a glance), and I grab the* inkin *(bell) which is my instrument for the entry ceremony to the zendo. The scent of incense and the rustle of robes nudge me into a dimension of stillness; Deb comes up on the left with the* hako *(incense box) holding the simmering charcoal, Howard holds the stick of incense in the middle, and I anchor our entry party on the right. And as we stand with our backs to the zendo facing our teacher, we formally begin our entry with three bows, and I punctuate each bow with the sound of the inkin. We turn and follow Jikyo Sensei into service, and on crossing the threshold of the zendo, we enter the world of spirit and community. . .*

Not everyone is moved by bells, chanting and incense, but one can find solace, metaphor and meaning in religious community. Community provides a sacred space, both literally and figuratively, where we can temporarily leave behind our obsessions with the day-to-day difficulties and focus on the infinite stretch of moments that present themselves to us, one after the other. As we practice at Three Treasures Zen Community, we have the luxury of combining the religious/communal activities, such as service and a dharma talk, with time for silent meditation and private interview with our teacher. What's precious for me is to be able to practice the religious ritual such as service, which is truly like a dance, choreographed for us to celebrate our lives and support us in our aspirations to know our true nature, along with the sitting meditation, where we quietly breathe life into each moment of stillness.

Ultimately, that is just what the combination of religious practice and spiritual practice sets out to do: to blend the best that we can learn and share in community, through our presence, participation and beliefs, with the fruits we harvest from our individual spiritual practices. The *religious practice* provides a belief system that has been tested through time for its integrity and universal meaning; it also provides communal activities, growth through relationship, sacred space and ritual. The *spiritual practice* provides the opportunity for ridding oneself of delusive thought and unifying the mind, and for connecting with the Divine energy. For many of us, combining the religious and spiritual practices provides the synergy for the deepest spirituality.

Religious Practice

In earlier chapters I explained that this book doesn't provide a comprehensive description of religious traditions; there are many books available, and many are listed at the end of this book, that can provide you with a wealth of information about the belief systems, sacred practices and doctrine of many different religions. Instead, I've described the most important and valuable aspects of religious practice (Chapter 2). What I haven't talked about are the life-changing choices that you may need to make in order to combine religious and spiritual practices as the framework and foundation of your life. The following section is mainly written for those who have been peripherally involved, or never involved, with a religious community. If this profile describes you, there are choices you may need to make that will help you decide whether you are willing or prepared to join a religious community. Among the most crucial of these choices are the following: (1) Facing your demons; (2) Knowing what you want and need from community, and recognizing what you have to offer; and (3) Making the commitment to community.

Facing Your Demons

Are you a person who has painful memories associated with religious community, or do you have friends or family who have shared their upsetting experiences with you? In no way do I want to discount the power of that pain; I've noticed, however, that people who have abandoned religious community talk as if it were an act of defiance—"I'll never put myself in that position again"—as if they were making sure they would never repeat that kind of hurtful experience. Many of the demons that people encountered were in the terrible pain of disillusionment and hurt that they associated with religious leaders or institutions or members of religious communities. They are determined to avoid future disappointment, shame, guilt, sadness or any emotional trauma that they or others experienced in a formal religious setting. The fact is, we encounter pain all the time, even though we do our best to avoid it. We focus most of our energies, consciously or unconsciously, on making sure that we never have to face our "demons" again, that people don't hurt us, that we don't screw up, and that we get our needs met, and darned if, in spite of all our efforts, we continue to be hurt, make mistakes and are disappointed.

Other people have simply become disenchanted with religion; as children, they were punished for their curiosity about the rules, or they were disappointed when practices that were supposedly inviolable were changed, or they realized that the formal religion did not fill their soul space; ultimately they left in anger, sadness or disillusionment. The unfortunate outcome of abandoning religious community altogether is that they've thrown out the baby with the bath water—they've deserted what may sometimes appear to be narrow-minded, rigid and self-serving organizations, but they've also given up the chance to be supported, to celebrate the Divine and their lives in community, and the opportunity to share their special gifts with others.

In Chapter 10 you'll learn about options that you might take to explore community, even if you've been dead-set against it for a long time. A key question to ask yourself is: am I willing to limit my spiritual growth by giving away my power to the past; do I want to continue to let my painful memories separate me from the richness and diversity of communal religious life?

Knowing What You Want, Need and Have to Offer

Sometimes people have unrealistic expectations of religious community. They expect the perfect community, perfect leadership, and perfect membership. When you explore community, you might expect the people to be inclusive and hospitable and, of course, you'll want to feel instantly comfortable. Many religious communities have many options for becoming better acquainted and for feeling included and involved: workshops, retreats, communal celebrations, small group activities (from prayer and meditation groups to singles and couples groups), and volunteer opportunities; you'll need to take the initiative to investigate what is available and make an effort to experiment with different opportunities to decide what you want and need, and to give what you have to offer.

I remember recently a new person came to our Zen center. As I walked in the door, someone introduced me to her, and I smiled and said "hi" and headed for the kitchen counter where I realized I had seen an earring the week before that I had lost but had not recognized as my own. (Don't ask…) Suddenly as I was rummaging through a drawer, Sensei caught my eye and gently said, "Susan, did you meet our guest?" I sheepishly stopped what I was doing, mumbled something about a lost earring, and took a few minutes to get acquainted. I'm not proud of my behavior, but we all tend to get absorbed in our monumental as well as trivial problems, and we forget that others have needs for inclusion and friendship.

When I first attended the Zen center, I kept expecting people to go out of their way to meet me; many were friendly, but were occasionally preoccupied in the way I described myself earlier. I realized that if I really wanted people to know me, I had to extend myself, reveal myself and contribute in some way. I volunteered for committees, made a point of speaking with different people and found out more about them, and they often reciprocated; eventually I became a member of the Board of Directors. Once I made the decision to be engaged at different levels, I never felt alone again.

Another unrealistic expectation is wanting people to exemplify the highest values of the religious practice, whether it's charity, love, or compassion, or any other virtue that we value. Rather than finding reasons to judge others silently, we might search our own hearts for those times when we, too, have failed to fulfill the morals and ethics of our belief systems, and reflect on them. We might also consider how we could guide and support others who are stumbling on the path to find their bearings and get back on track.

People in religious community might demonstrate most of the positive values that we admire, but those same people may have characteristics that drive us crazy. Whether it's the person who talks too much, or the one who seems aloof, or the one who's always late, or the one who gossips, or the one who criticizes (or add any other negative attribute that makes you nuts), we tend to make those people the focus of our harshest judgments about community, and use them to justify our decisions not to participate. The funny thing is, those very people can be wonderful sources of a religious/spiritual practice. Kay Lindahl, Executive Director of the Alliance for Spiritual Community told me, "I've developed a practice of appreciating those who really irritate me, and that's been an amazing experience in and of itself, to just say, 'oh that's Mary being Mary, how could she be anyone else but Mary,' then I can hear what she has to say. But if I'm irritated because Mary's being Mary (laughter), I won't hear anything she's said, because I'll be fighting it."

Another area where we might be disappointed is expecting the religious community to fulfill all our spiritual needs and aspirations. As I've said earlier, community is a precious part of spiritual development, but it may not be sufficient for nurturing a profoundly intimate relationship with the Divine or the cosmos. The only way you may achieve that connection is through a personal practice, which will be nurtured and ripened by your relationships with others.

Making a Commitment

Let's look at "time" first—who wants to spend perhaps the limited leisure time that one has cooped up in a church, synagogue or center? Frankly, I do. In my case, going to the Zen center takes up a Tuesday evening, with over an hour of driving and two hours of sitting and walking meditation (with an extra half-hour thrown in if we have service that night). I never see this as a burden—that doesn't mean it's not tough to go down there sometimes, that there are evenings I'd much rather stretch out on the sofa with a glass of wine and a good mystery novel—but those times are rare. To me, going to the Zen center is a respite from the every day, a chance to mingle and share meditation time with people I care about. I also experience Tuesday nights the same way I see getting dressed in the morning—I never ask myself whether I should go outside without putting some clothes on—I just dress. When my motivation for sitting practice is sagging, sitting with this group of people buoys me up, strengthens my practice. I'm comforted in knowing that others in my community share my belief that life is sometimes painful and that we suffer, and the path we have taken guides us in liberating ourselves and others from the suffering we experience in life. And my life is richer for the goals and aspirations that we share.

You might also put a high value on your independence. "Commitment" to a religious community may sound like an infringement upon your freedom to do whatever you like, whenever you feel like it. Paradoxically, commitment both infringes upon and enhances your freedom. If you make a commitment to show up at a religious center, church or synagogue, you are giving up your freedom to be somewhere else. As my spiritual life deepens, I am learning that there is no freedom to be compared to the liberation that one experiences when one pierces the curtain of life's illusions and sheds the bondage of a superficial and meaningless existence. What would be authentic freedom for you?

Only you can decide whether you are truly ready to integrate religious community into your spiritual life. That means waking up on a given morning and not asking whether you really feel like attending a religious meeting or not; it means remembering that you have chosen a life of spirit and community, and that there's a whole group of people waiting to uplift you and to whom you can provide support. Sister Jane DeLisle of the Center for Spiritual Development in Orange, California, says about community, "You can do more together than you can ever do alone; I can go to church, I don't want to be there, I'm in the pits, and don't care about anybody or anything; I'm just out of it. On a day like that, the faith of the community carries me, and on a day that you feel that way, the faith of the community carries you. So it's not a matter of what you can get out of it; it's what we can do and be for each other, because we're not called to be alone; we're called to be one."

To be part of community also means that there are things you may have to give up to make time for community. I know people have a lot of demands on their lives, but I'm also baffled at the amount of time people spend on activities that even they admit are a waste of time, but they are unwilling to give up. My priorities are clear: time with my husband (particularly since he travels a lot), time for my work, time for my friends, and time for my practice (which really embraces my husband, my work and my friends); everything else is low on my priority list. Take inventory; make choices; give stuff up. When the spirit calls you, don't tell it you're busy watching a ten-part mini-series; just answer.

What's important here is that community provides fertile ground for spiritual development; the opportunity for us to expand upon our expectations instead of limit them, to share our hopes and dreams rather than abandon them, and to uplift the community and be supported by it, are the spiritual gifts that can be tended and shared. And they can only be found, through relationships, in community.

Spiritual Practice

My friend Howard and I were involved in a group discussion at our Zen center recently regarding the practice of ritual in community. Howard said that in looking at the various kinds of practices, "It's like having ice cream. Sometimes I prefer chocolate, sometimes I get vanilla, and sometimes I have strawberry. It isn't that one is better than another, it's just that we all have our preferences." We burst into laughter at the simple truth of his statement.

Unlike religious practices, which are framed within specific belief systems and practices, many spiritual practices transcend religious boundaries, and can be used as tools for spiritual practice across religions. For that reason, in this section I describe a variety of spiritual practices whose origins rest in one tradition, but are functional within and complementary to many others.

In developing personal spiritual practices, you'll have preferences and comfort levels, what works for you, and what doesn't. The Rev. Lois McAfee with the Ministry of Spiritual Formation, and the Rev. Preston Price with the United Methodist Church of Garden Grove, California, both of them Spiritual Directors, addressed the importance of matching temperament to spiritual practices. Rev. McAfee says,

> Spiritual practices that work have partly to do with personality types; we're getting to know that no one form fits all, no linear way fits all. Certain things work for me that don't work for my husband, but we parallel in our practices in some ways. If we are at all open and God is certainly quite willing, we will discover practices that lead to mutual, prayerful engagement. Usually in the course of our lives, perhaps also developmentally related, our prayer life jumps around. We become aware that our prayer has lost its vitality; when the prayer form doesn't work anymore, it is time to experiment with others. If I spend more time staring out the window than reading the scriptures from the daily lectionary on my lap, and if I find the former a transcendent and em-powering experience, that is probably my prayer form for now. My hunger for prayer through scripture will return in its time. We must be flexible enough to go where the Spirit invites us, and to be attentive for such movements.

Pastor Price adds, "I think spiritual practice is at its best when you're open to what floats your boat, whether it's Christian, Jewish, Buddhist or others. If it connects you, then do it for gosh sakes; don't worry about what kind of prayer, just go with that."

On the other hand, you might consider doing a practice that complements, rather than matches your temperament. I happen to like sitting meditation precisely because it is counter to my tempera-ment: I'm active and busy, and meditation helps me slow down, al-lows me to center myself and open to the possibilities of connecting with Spirit.

Swami Sarvadevananda, of the Vedanta Society of Southern Cali-fornia, describes how Vedanta (a major school of Hinduism) provides multiple ways for people to find connection with God: "Some people like meditation and will sit for hours. If someone is intellectual, he or she can study and understand why we are here and investigate all the intricacies of the philosophies. Even devotion is one path in the holistic life, so when you talk of devotion, you are driven to love God, you have to cry for him, you have to pray for him."

By creating your individual spiritual practice, you have the opportunity to experience life at a deeper and more profound level. Father Brad Karelius of the Episcopal Church of the Messiah in Santa Ana, California explains it this way: "We can experience God as very present in our lives right now; it's not just an idea, but a presence we can be in communion with, and there are various disciplines that can help us with that." Instead of only *believing in* a Divine or universal presence, we *experience* that presence. Our lives become more than just measuring our actions and behaviors against beliefs and proscriptions; instead, we experience the desire to be guided by and infused with those beliefs and with love, to manifest that love in service, and to be in relationship with that which is greater and more profound. Even when we struggle with our darker natures, our obsessions and desires, we have access to the Divine in ourselves.

Sister Jane DeLisle gave me one of my favorite terms, "soul space"; she believes that formal religion leads to the spiritual:

> The religion without the spiritual makes no sense. We're all spiritual beings by our nature; if we only focus on the religion or the community, we find ourselves hungering for a more intimate connection with God. We also can't live totally out of ego, because there's another part of us being denied if we only hold on to the ego: we limit our ability to deepen our relationship with God and to fill our soul space. That's why the spiritual is so important.

So we will explore what it means to fill that soul space, describing various spiritual practices that will help you dissolve the separation that you may be experiencing between yourself and the Other, between your life and the rest of existence.

For this book, spiritual practices have been defined as *those activities which guide and assist people in making a more intimate connection with the Divine or universal.* Although most spiritual practices are individual practices, some of them are practiced in religious community. Rather than divide practices as religious or spiritual, I have defined them as *active, receptive* and *everyday practices. Active prac-*

tices are those activities that require action on your part; you'll learn about chanting, movement, fasting, walking meditation, journaling and retreats. *Receptive practices* are passive practices that are done without activity and in silence such as prayer and meditation. *Everyday practices* involve transforming daily events such as washing dishes, cooking and listening, into spiritual activities.

Active Practices

These activities offer a kind of celebration of your life in relation to the Other that you can do on your own or in community. They are especially helpful for people who are uncomfortable starting a spiritual practice in stillness. They provide the counterbalance for receptive practices, a contrast between quietly opening up, becoming a receptacle for the Divine or the All, and actively appealing to and rejoicing in Spirit.

Chanting

Two wonderful experiences I have had in chanting confirmed that it is a heartfelt way of my praising the Infinite, and actively inviting It into my life. One experience took place at a Jewish Meditation Conference in Los Angeles. We had a few opportunities to sing, and when a song was repeated over and over, it became a chant. Rabbi Shefa Gold composed a chant based on Genesis 27:17, which in English reads, "How Awesome is this Place," or in some translations, "How Awesome is God." The Hebrew transliteration is "Mah Norah Hamakome Hazeh."

There were a couple of hundred of us, at least, seated in the synagogue where the conference was being held, and Shefa taught us the chant in three parts and accompanied us with a drum and her sweet voice. As my own voice blended with this moving ocean of song ,it was a most exhilarating and moving experience, as we all sang our parts and proclaimed our sense of awe and happiness in those sacred moments. I sang with my eyes closed and let the waves of rhapsody sweep over me, feeling myself immersed in a chorus that was calling out to the Divine in sweet harmony. We sang and sang, and after a time we heard Shefa bringing us to closure by slowly singing one last verse. We stopped and breathed in the energy created by our song, followed by a textured stillness that cloaked us all as one.

There is a quality of chant and song that moves me in a way that no other practice does. I feel as if I am opening my heart to the One and saying here I am, rejoicing in Your Presence, let me know You. I'm not a singer by any means, but I don't think God cares. I believe it's my sincerity that counts.

Father John McAndrew shares how we have we have separated ourselves from song:

> We live in a culture that unfortunately has divided itself into people who sing and people who don't, most of whom don't. I remember the images from Nelson Mandela's inauguration, tens of thousands of African men, not women, men, chanting and dancing. Now where did we lose *our* voice? This last week-end [where he facilitated an Alcoholics Anonymous retreat] I taught guys a simple round, and when we started the round, they were all smiling like second graders, because we love to sing as kids, but somewhere along the line we stopped. I think we can reclaim that as a spiritual practice, and coming together we can make sound, we can make a prayer, that I can't make myself.

Another moving experience I've had with chant was at St. Anselm of Canterbury Episcopal Church in Garden Grove, California, whose rector is Father Wilfredo Benitez. On the first Thursday of every month, he facilitates a small group that participates in Taize, a type of chant that originated with the ecumenical community of Taize, France. Father Wilfredo has designed the hour so that there are 7-8 minutes of silent meditation, then 7-8 minutes singing a chant, then 7-8 minutes of meditation and 7-8 minutes of another chant, and so on, so that there are four periods during the hour combining meditation and chant. The chants are short and simple, sometimes in Latin and sometimes in English. For example, "Bless the Lord my soul and bless God's holy name, Bless the Lord my soul, Who leads me into life" is one typical chant. I can't adequately describe what takes place, but can only say that with each successive period of chant and meditation, there is a deepness and fullness of experience, of stillness and openness, of receptivity and peace, that is, for me, unique to the chanting experience.

Movement

Sacred dance is another expressive mode of experiencing the spirit in one's life. Sometimes at our intensive meditation retreats at the Zen center, Jikyo Sensei leads us through sacred songs and dances. As we sing and dance, we connect with the sacred through our senses. We hear, we see, we touch; at times we connect through our eyes, sometimes through our voices, and through our hands, and when we do, our spirits touch each other. One of my favorite dances and chants is, "The earth she is our mother, we must take care of her, the earth she is our mother, we must take care of her, re-unite my people, be one, re-unite my people, be one." One can take each phrase, even a single word and make it a meditation, a way of remembering how we are all interconnected, of one body, from one source.

The Rev. Murray Finck begins his active practice early in the day: "I like to begin the day when it's still dark. I light a candle, and go into a quiet room where it's just myself and the one little light. I spend about a half an hour just doing hatha yoga, and then I spend time in six different prayer postures, quietly, with a little background music and that one single light." The Rev. Finck then progresses into other spiritual practices to complete his morning disciplines.

Pastor Preston Price also has done a great deal of sacred dance. He has worked with a youth in his United Methodist community to design a dance for a song the congregation is already singing, with the words, "God will raise you up on eagle's wings, bear you on the breath of dawn, make you to shine like the sun and hold you in the palm of His hand." As he recited these words, I felt myself uplifted by this moving imagery.

Fasting

Most religions include fasting as a part of their religious practices, but I'm including it in the section on spiritual practices because it requires a special kind of individual discipline and commitment. In these times, many of us in the Western world don't know what it means to go hungry. We are conditioned to feeding our desires, and often do not reflect on the source of our pleasures; for example, instead of expressing our gratitude, we take for granted the farmers who grow our food, the grocery stores that stock it, and our modern kitchens where we prepare it.

Islam provides a very profound way of reflecting on the source of our sustenance, on the source of our very lives. In Islam, the most holy month of the year is the period of Ramadan. During this time, the Prophet Muhammad received his initial revelation and ten years later made his historic trip from Mecca to Medina. To honor this period, devout and able Muslims neither eat food nor drink, from dawn until after sundown, when they may eat in moderation. Dr. Muzzamil Siddiqi, Director of the Islamic Society of Orange County explains, "During Ramadan you may feel very hungry or thirsty, or both. But then you ask, 'what is the purpose of my life; do I just exist for eating and drinking, or for something else?' So this changes your perspective; you realize, 'I am not the servant of food, I am not the servant of my work; I am the servant of God, and anything can wait, but I have to do my duty to the One who has given me everything.'"

Walking Meditation

Walking meditation takes many forms. When we sit for three, 30-minute periods at the Zen center, those periods are interspersed with ten minutes of kinhin, a walking meditation. I begin to walk with the rest of the community in a slow walk, which I match to my breath; I often take two breaths per step, to help me slow down and pay attention. After a few minutes of slow walking, the *jikido* or time keeper hits the wooden clackers and we walk quickly. Walking meditation is a great way to maintain our attentive minds and spiritual practice in the middle of activity—what many of us aspire to do in everyday life.

We have multiple opportunities to do walking meditation every day, whether we're walking up and down stairs, from our cars to our offices, from our offices to the water cooler. Each time we walk, we can make a deliberate attempt to be fully present in the moment, hearing the rustle of our dresses or feeling the brushing of our pants legs, noticing the pace and length of our steps. Every time we walk, we have the chance to see those moments not as an empty span of meaningless time, but as an occasion to fully connect with the unfolding tapestry of our lives.

A number of people interviewed spoke of their experiences in walking the labyrinth, another ancient practice. One evening at St. Anselm of Canterbury Episcopal Church we finished Taize in the church's library and prepared to walk the courtyard labyrinth. My friend Connie joined me for the evening's experience.

As we enter the hallway outside of the study where we've chanted Taize, I introduce Father Wilfredo to Connie, and he tells us that Thich Chon Tanh (whom everyone calls Thay), a local Buddhist monk and teacher, will be coming to walk the labyrinth, too. He says Thay walks very slowly, so we can wait or we can begin. I wave to Connie and we approach the entry to the labyrinth; I give her my best instructions or, better said, best guess, of how to walk the labyrinth, and we begin. Thay arrives shortly thereafter with three other guests, and with Father Wilfredo and two of our Taize chanters, we begin our journey through the labyrinth.

I begin to walk slowly and self-consciously as I lead the group, and the evening curtain of darkness settles around us. Gradually, I walk a little faster, but only because my body bows to the rhythm of my breath—breathe in, one step, breathe out, one step. As I walk the path that resembles the plaits of a woven rug gone mad, I move by each sojourner following the teasing trail, at times wondering how far away from the center we are. As we pass one another through the winding maze, shoulders touch, sleeves catch, and at times we slightly turn our shoulders in synchronized rhythm to keep a brushing shoulder from being a bump. I breathe, I step, I breathe, I step…I notice that Father Wilfredo steps from the labyrinth as the sprinklers come on, and he turns them off and brushes the water from our paths. He leaves twice to clear our path, and each time rejoins us. Our journey takes us from one side of the courtyard to the other, and at times I realize I don't know which side of the courtyard I am on, and don't try to figure it out, since all that matters is one breath, one step, one breath, one step, contemplative souls passing through shadows. We've formed a community of seekers, winding with the mysterious path which we have not designed, and whose bends we cannot anticipate. But we walk, alone and together in this space, the fountain splashing, the incense drifting, accompanied part-time by music floating from the church, other times by silence. One breath, one step. I wonder how long we've walked, think I am walking too slowly but can only follow my own internal rhythm which transcends my need to "do it right." One by one, we finally enter the center of the labyrinth. We move around the center's edges, and wait for each person to complete his or her journey. And then the journey is over, and everyone silently speaks to the moment in his or her own way. I peek to notice some heads bowed, some hands raised above heads, all standing quietly. And then suddenly we acknowledge with smiles and shy glances that we have completed the path; Father Wilfredo hugs those around him, and I return his hug in gratitude and companionship. It is late; we spent one hour walking into the labyrinth. I leave, crossing over the once bewildering patterns and pass into real life once again.

Walking a labyrinth takes me into the space of "not-knowing"; how often I think I know where I am going, and believe I'm about to arrive at my objective, only to be surprised by another turn away from my intended destination, as I am moved in an unexpected direction. As Father Wilfredo says, "Part of the beauty of contemplation is that it doesn't require any thought process, and the further you get away from that, the better it is. The labyrinth helps you focus in that way; when you're walking the path, it's easier to focus on that moment, the present moment, and it opens you up to experiencing the profound and mystical."

Journaling

Journaling is a spiritual practice that allows us to connect with Spirit by reflecting on our lives and asking for guidance. Sister Jane DeLisle teaches journaling and uses it to review with God the experiences of her life. "Journaling for me is a meditative practice and it's more than that; it helps me to take life experience, write about that and move deeper with it. When I'm reviewing an experience, I ask God, pray to Jesus, about what the experience should mean to me. Then I write my reaction, as if I were talking to Him, and let the flow of the pen be His response."

Pastor Preston Price also uses journalling as a spiritual tool. "It's not like keeping a journal, it's more about writing an ongoing letter to God, like writing a prayer. Usually I write about three times larger than I usually do, so I don't worry about my handwriting; it keeps me focused, and I have less free association. A number of times, the most productive process has been when I've set up a conversation with me and God, and I write both sides of the conversation, and there've been some amazing breakthroughs: 'God, why are you doing this, what in the world is going on,' and then writing the response and, oh my gosh, it's the discovery of something that wasn't in me before, that I hadn't seen or heard before but comes pouring out."

I've started to do my own journaling, and I've felt awkward at times. At other times, I'm surprised at what comes out, and it truly does not sound like my own voice or thoughts. Whether I'm writing God's words or am simply inspired by the Infinite, I'm grateful for the wisdom that I encounter in those authored moments.

Retreat

The last active practice, which actually can include both active and receptive practices and individual and communal activities, is the retreat. I have attended several retreats over the last seven years, from one day "sits" to one week intensive retreats. There are also retreats that run from one to three months or longer.

The purposes of a retreat may be defined in many ways, depending on the religious community sponsoring it. A retreat allows me to deepen my spiritual practice and, therefore, my life: through attentiveness to every activity whether it is eating, meditating, serving others, work practice, talking with a teacher, or participating in religious service, I have an environment that supports my experiencing life in its richness from one moment to the next; it allows me to go deeply into those places where I am stuck or hurt, and to explore them from a place of love and care. The results of a retreat are difficult to measure in everyday life, but for me, they manifest in my responding to those I love and work with in more compassionate and powerful ways.

I'm at a one-week Zen sesshin (retreat), and I get myself up at 4:20 a.m. so I can sneak in a quick shower and allow travel time; members of the community have kindly opened their home to me, and I only have a seven-minute commute to the Zen center. I'm on the road by 4:50 a.m., abandoning any hope or desire to style my hair or put on make-up. By 5:00 a.m. I am in waiting for Sensei, since she has invited me to be her jisha (attendant), which is an honor and a challenge. I've been secretly and kindly coached by a senior practitioner who tells me that I can choose to do only what the Sensei asks me to do, or I can be "mother" to the Sensei who has the most demanding routine of all of us. I decide that being a mother and pampering her sounds like much more fun, and am delighted to scrap my Western preconceptions about servitude; this is not about servitude, but about service.

The day is filled with making sure Sensei has whatever she needs, and better yet, anticipating any need she might have. I've gotten so tuned in, that one time when Sensei says she'll be busy for ten or 15 minutes, I sit on my zafu (pillow) and suddenly I know it's time to get up. As I patter from the zendo, I startle her in the hallway as she's coming to find me, and she asks how I knew she was ready; I just shrug my shoulders and smile.

My main job is helping to light all the altars in the morning, and arranging for people to have interviews with Sensei, all the while maintaining my attention to my practice in the present moment. Every opportunity I have to sit on my zafu without interruption is one I relish, and yet the task of maintaining my con-

templative and mindful composure within activity is a growth experience. (I can't say I mind stretching my legs during the approximately eight hours of meditation per day.) The long periods of meditation are punctuated by short periods of service, work practice, and oryoki (a ritual practice of eating meals). Although there are sometimes agonizing periods of remorse during some retreats—how could I have signed up for a week of this??—this retreat becomes one of deepening practice and maturation. I experience how rich a spiritual practice of service can be, and appreciate that maintaining mindfulness in the midst of activity is an ideal that I can aspire to in my everyday life.

Combining the Religious and Spiritual

There are specific practices that are both religious and spiritual. One example is when I light the Friday night candles to usher in the Sabbath. I find this a deeply moving experience, celebrating this gift that God has given us: the day of rest. In the Jewish tradition, the entire week centers on the Sabbath, either winding down from Sabbath or working towards it.

On Friday morning I arrange two candles and candlesticks in preparation for Friday evening. As close to sunset as possible, I light the candles; then I draw my hands around the candles and toward my face three times, and then cover my eyes. I take a moment of stillness to open my heart to the One Infinite; then I recite the blessing: Blessed art Thou, Oh Lord our God, King of the Universe, Who has made us holy by Your Commandments and commanded us to kindle the Sabbath candles. I take a breath and open my eyes, and as if for the first time, see the light from the candles that ushers in the Sabbath Queen, the Sabbath Bride, the feminine and receptive side of the Divine spirit that illuminates the world.

Another religious and spiritual practice combination mentioned by many of those interviewed was the sacrament of the Holy Eucharist. The Rev. Charlotte Cleghorn, an Episcopal priest and a spiritual director, describes the Eucharist in this way:

> In the Episcopal church, the Holy Eucharist is the foretaste of the heavenly banquet, when this world as we know it comes to an end, and people are seated in heaven and will eat together as Jesus feeds us. It is also the principal office celebrated on Sunday, because every Sunday is a 'little Easter,' so we celebrate Christ's presence with us through the bread and wine in remembrance of his last meal with his disciples. It's the principal feast around which we gather, and there is something very powerful for me as a priest, when I see people coming up to receive the bread and wine. In some traditions you sit; in our tradition you come forward, and there's something very powerful about coming and kneeling or standing and putting your empty hands out and the priest puts the host in your hand and says "the body of Christ, the bread of heaven"; we talk about the real presence of Christ, that somehow Christ is really present in that bread and wine, but how we don't know, that's the mystery, and so we take that in, the mystery that is also believing; and it is nurturing and nourishing us, symbolically but also literally.

There are hundreds, perhaps thousands of rituals in religious practice that allow us to connect with our soul space, to bridge the separation between our everyday living and the Oneness. As Rabbi Robbins of Congregation N'vay Shalom in Los Angeles says, "The ceremonies are not things in themselves; they are the means by which we enliven and enlighten our lives, and provide the meaning; and they draw God's presence into the world, so that ceremonies are gateways, and we draw God's presence through the gateway, and that transforms us."

Receptive Practices

In writing about receptive practices, we focus on those tools that are done primarily individually and in stillness. Since meditation and prayer are closely related, I will address them as one category, and indicate when each can be practiced. Since there are a lot of misconceptions about meditation, however, I'm going to spend some time explaining what meditation is and is not.

The Practice of Meditation

In his book, *Mindfulness in Plain English*, the Venerable Henepola Gunaratana addresses the misconceptions and facts about meditation. The Venerable says,

> Meditation is certainly not an irrelevant practice strictly for ascetics and hermits. It is a practical skill that focuses on everyday events and has immediate application in everybody's life. Meditation is not other-worldly. Unfortunately, this very fact constitutes the drawback for certain students. They enter the practice expecting instantaneous cosmic revelation, complete with angelic choirs. What they usually get is a more efficient way to take out the trash and better ways to deal with Uncle Herman. They are needlessly disappointed. The trash solution comes first. The voices of archangels take a bit longer."[1]

Other misconceptions include the belief that meditation is mysterious and can't be understood; that meditation is dangerous, and should be avoided; that it is used to avoid reality or get high; that after a couple of weeks of meditation, all our problems go away. All of these are misconceptions about the art of meditation.

Meditation, depending on the type you practice, is not only about concentration, but can also be about becoming more mindful, more present in the moment. It is a tool which, over time, can cut through delusive thought, to help us see our lives more clearly, to dissolve the separation between ourselves and the Other. Although some people have powerful spiritual experiences, many of us learn that to simply be able to observe one's life-giving breath, and to be present to that miracle, is a spiritual gift.

In a society where people like "fast food" results, however, meditation doesn't play well. Meditation is not an easy practice for most people, particularly when they realize how truly out of control their minds are. Many people steer away from meditation because they like instant success in their practices; however, experienced meditation practitioners know that some days they are deeply present and alive

---

1. Venerable Henepola Gunaratana, *Mindfulness in Plain English* (Boston: Wisdom Publications, 1992), p.27.

and focused in their meditations, and other times, in spite of their best efforts, the demanding person at work gets almost all of their attention during meditation, and they spend most of their time noticing their distracting thoughts and their frustration; with practice, they learn to just keep coming back to the focus of their meditation. I remember hearing a delightful and insightful talk by Peter Vidmar, the world-class gymnast, who talked about how gymnasts practice over and over and over again, the best of them never losing sight of their goals. That's what you do in meditation (and why we call it practice), because when you meditate and are continually distracted by your thoughts, you just keep coming back to your point of focus, without self-criticism or anger, whether your focus is prayer, or koans, the Divine, or the breath. I have an incredibly busy mind—a favorite term of "monkey mind" doesn't do it justice! And yet I love my meditation practice, and am in awe of how it continues to deepen my spiritual life.

There are a few books on meditation in the bibliography, but here are a few basic instructions for meditation if you'd like to get started:

- Choose a regular time for your meditation—morning or evening or when you're the least likely to be interrupted.
- Pick a regular place to meditate that is quiet and comfortable. Try to make the space special, so that it helps to feed your spirit; flowers, pictures and candles can help create sacred space.
- Start with a short sitting period. When I attended my first meditation workshop, I sat up to 15 minutes; I maintained that level for several months, before increasing it. Don't over-commit.
- You can sit on a chair or on the floor. If you sit in a chair, try to sit straight without leaning on the back of the chair— you don't have to arch your back. If your feet don't touch the floor, find something to put under your feet so that your legs bend at about a 90 degree angle and your back muscles don't have to strain.
- If you are sitting on the floor, use a firm pillow under your bottom and sit on the front third, so that you are tilted slightly forward. Sit with your back straight. You can try a half lotus,

which is done with both knees on the floor and one foot lying on the calf of the other leg, or a full lotus where both knees touch the floor and each foot lies on the calf of the opposite leg. Since most of us have bodies that refuse to even consider these positions, you can sit Burmese style, which allows both knees to lie on the floor, with one foot in front of the other. A fourth choice is called *seiza*, which is a Japanese form of sitting. Use a firm pillow standing on end, and sit so that your buttocks are on the pillow, and rest your buttocks on your heels. Whichever style you choose, it's important to sit straight, because straight sitting reduces fatigue. Try to get a sense of lining up your ears, shoulders and hips; then check the alignment of your eyes, chin and belly button. Rather than arch your back to pull up your body (since gravity is persistent about dragging us down), imagine that your head or clavicle is being pulled upward by a string; this thought usually helps to straighten the body without strain.

Once you find a sitting position, place your hands so that they rest comfortably, with the back of one hand resting comfortably in the palm of the other. You may sit with eyes open or closed, but some teachers recommend keeping them open and looking at the floor three to five feet in front of you (without tipping your head) with an unfocused gaze. To keep saliva from accumulating in your mouth, place the tip of your tongue against the back of your front teeth and swallow.

In the section *Simple Meditation*, you will find some basic meditations to practice. Keep in mind that there is much more to learn about meditation and its complexities. I encourage you to read up and give it a try.

Meditation, Prayer and Silence

At this time in my spiritual life, I am following two spiritual paths: Judaism and Zen Buddhism. I've chosen to select time and space to practice each separately, although each practice, I believe, is complementary to the other. At different times in this section, I will show how I fulfill my Jewish practice and my Zen practice. In addition, you will learn about the practices of others, why they have selected those practices, and how these approaches deepen their spiritual lives.

I'm a person who likes to be busy, and I'm also pretty verbal. So sitting in silence has had a profound effect on my spiritual nature, because I balance *doing* with *being*. Pastor Craig Lockwood of Vineyard Christian Fellowship in Anaheim, California says, "There's a need to differentiate between my being and my doing. What I do can flow out of who I am, or it can flow out of my performance, but there's a big difference: because who I *am* is mostly formed in my *contemplation* or my *being*, not out of what I *do*." Rabbi Jonathan Omer-Man, founder and Rabbi Emeritus for Metivta, A Center for Contemplative Judaism in Los Angeles is a strong advocate of stillness. Rabbi Omer-Man says, "The place of silence is where God dwells. Why silence? Because in spite of all our heartfelt wishes, the presence of the Divine is extremely subtle. Any noise and you can't hear it. Any inner drama and you can't feel it. Any powerful ideas or passions and it's not there. The field in which our experience of the Divine exists is of silence." Jan Hoffman, a Quaker, describes a receptive practice that happens in community, called "waiting worship" or "open worship":

> A typical meeting of worship occurs on Sunday. We begin in silence and sometimes that silence continues for the entire meeting—no one speaks. After attending many meetings for worship, however, we begin to recognize different kinds of silence. We call a meeting "gathered" at the point where we feel caught up in divine energy and joined together in it. We call it "covered" if we have experienced a particular sense of God speaking to us more deeply, which does not happen every week. At other times the silence will have been very shallow, and we will not have gone deep.
>
> Out of the silence, anyone may speak as led by the Spirit. There is no human leader, so everyone is responsible for being faithful to speak a message as it is given to him or her. We also have a sense that while there is one message to be given to the meeting that morning, it will be offered through several people. Quite frequently, a person will rise and speak the words given, and it doesn't make sense to them and doesn't seem to be finished, but the Spirit says, "stop" and the person sits down. Then another speaker will take up where the first one left off, so that

the message gradually unfolds as each person speaks—to our great wonder. When such a harmonious message emerges, we feel it as a gift of grace, a "covered" meeting.

There are also meetings for worship where people rise to speak not from the Spirit's nudging, but from their own egos. We sometimes call these meetings "popcorn" meetings, since one speaker's words are unconnected to another's—they just pop out randomly. In this case, there is no unified message, and we do not feel that gift of grace. Instead we try to learn from these times how to discern more clearly the Spirit's work in us and to be more faithful to its movement.

Although I love to celebrate the Divine through chant or dance, I experience relationship with God in my moments of silent meditation and prayer. That sense of intimacy is subtle, but nevertheless present for me. The following sections describe both my Jewish and Zen practices.

My Practices

I do my Jewish meditation in the morning. I meditate in my office and in a chair, which is a way of distinguishing between my Jewish practice and Zen practice. (When practicing Zen I sit on a pillow on the floor in another room. At some level I've felt that I want to maintain the integrity of each practice, so although the two are complementary in many ways, I work with them separately.)

First, I choose a breath meditation, either breathing in the presence of God, or breathing in one of God's names. (In Judaism, God has 88 names.) After I have meditated for 15-20 minutes, I do the prayer called the *Modah Ani* in Hebrew, which states, "I thank You with gratitude, for returning my soul to me with compassion; great is Your faith." I contemplate this prayer, sometimes focusing on one word, such as gratitude or compassion, and sometimes praying the full and profound meaning, as I understand it. When I feel that I have fully experienced the prayer, I move to personal prayers for the health and wellbeing of family, other loved ones, and all those who may need healing in the world, as well as for myself; I don't ask God to remove my illnesses, but rather to heal my heart, and to give me the strength to deal with the maladies I am experiencing. When I finish, I spend

10 to 20 minutes journalling whatever comes up for me.

At night, before I go to sleep, I have four prayers I contemplate. At the encouragement of Rabbi Omer-Man, I first recall each person during the day who may have hurt or disappointed me and forgive them, and I then ask for forgiveness regarding each person I may have harmed. Then I meditate on the Shema in Hebrew, which reads "Hear O Israel, the Lord our God, the Lord is One." I then proceed to one of my favorite prayers, that is perhaps one of the most beautiful prayers in Hebrew. It is called by its first word, the *V'Ahavta*, or in English, "And you shall love . . ." and to me, it is a love note from and to God.

> And you shall love the Lord Your God, with all your heart, with all your soul, and with all your might. And these words which I command you this day shall be upon your heart. Teach them diligently to your children and speak of them while you sit in your house, while you walk on the way, when you retire, and when you arise. Bind them as a sign upon your arm and let them be tefillin between your eyes. And write them upon the doorposts of your house and upon your gates.

Finally, I end with the last line of a prayer called the *Adon Olam,* which says, "And I will rest my soul in your hands when I go to sleep, and then I will arise; my Spirit will remain with my body, *the Lord is with me, I shall not fear.*" Those last words are on my lips as I go to sleep.

This practice, which may change over time, has helped me reconnect with my Jewish tradition and with the Divine, and I feel gratitude for, peace with, and closeness to God as I do it. Sure, there are some days when my mind is an angry caged animal, and gratitude is a distant memory, so I breathe in and watch my anger and frustration; as I breathe with whatever comes up, and watch each thought as it invades my equanimity, it passes away on its own and I am left with my breath, spirit and stillness.

For those who desire a spiritual practice that focuses the mind and clarifies your life, a form of Zen meditation or *zazen,* might work for you. I have a room set aside (which is my husband's study when he is in town) where I keep my sitting pillow and rakasu. I also have a little altar with symbols of my spiritual practice. I prefer doing my

Zen practice in the evening, long enough after dinner for the food to settle, and early enough so that I won't fall asleep. I have worked with counting my breath (which can be done in several different ways that I'll describe later), koan practice, which is a form of working with the intuitive mind to understand a parable or question, and simply following my in and out breath.

Currently I am working with a mindfulness practice that focuses on the breath. After I get oriented on my sitting pillow on the floor, I take a deep breath and let it out very slowly; I do this three times, letting my mind and body settle. Then I do a body scan, starting with the *hara*, which is just below the belly button; as I take a breath, I notice how and if different parts of my body respond to each breath. I focus my breath and attention, moving up my body, noticing with each breath if and how my body responds; once I've gone up the front of my body, I go down my back, all the way to my toes. This only takes a few minutes, but it helps me to focus and integrate my body, mind and attention. The purpose of mindfulness practice is really to train the mind to be in the present moment. Since most of us spend the vast majority of our conscious moments being anywhere other than present, this is a profound experience of understanding how the mind works and learning how to be genuinely engaged in present time.

Although some people might question how I am able to maintain two spiritual practices, I can only say that it is deeply rewarding. Both practices complement each other and have enhanced my spiritual life immeasurably. And I am immensely grateful for two teachers who support me on my journey.

Simple Meditation

Before reading this section, be sure to review *The Practice of Meditation* section on how to choose a sitting position. Once you have done that, a form of counting your breath is a good way to begin. There are three that you might want to try:

1. Counting the in breath and the out breath—be certain that the breath leads, not the counting—this involves counting your first inhale with the number one, then counting the exhale as

the number two, and so on, until you reach ten. Then begin again with the number one. If you're just starting out, you may find your mind wanders right away. Each time your mind wanders, notice the thought (and do not judge or criticize yourself for becoming distracted), and as you watch it dissolve, go back to the number one. You may find that your mind is frequently distracted; this is normal and human, and it's how you work with your mind that counts. The purpose of meditation is not to have a blank mind or get rid of all your thoughts; it is to be able to be fully present to whatever arises.

2. You can count just the inhale or just the exhale of your breath, counting from one to ten. Then follow the rest of the procedure under #1 above for working with distractions.

3. You can count each inhale and exhale from one to ten, and then count each inhale and exhale the next time from ten to one, and alternate counting up or down with each set of ten breaths. Then work with distractions as described in #1.

The purpose of counting the breath is to give your mind something to grasp other than your wildly rampant thoughts. As you progress in your meditation, you may find that you prefer not to count, and that simply following your breath or meditating on a prayer, or another meditative practice suits you.

Koan Practice

Koans are unique to Zen practice. Koans can run from one sentence to several paragraphs, and often seem to be unsolvable riddles or puzzles, until we penetrate their depths to reveal their truths. A fairly well known koan is, "What is the sound of one hand clapping?" My very first koan was, "A monk asked Joshu in all earnestness, 'What is the meaning of the patriarch's coming from the West?' Joshu answered, 'The oak tree in the garden.'"

Too often, particularly in western society, we give a great deal of importance to cognitive thinking, comprehension, and problem-solving. Although this kind of thinking is valuable and essential for everyday life, there are many other ways of perceiving and understanding.

Koan practice must be done with a Zen Buddhist teacher, because as we meditate on a koan to try to dive into the depths of our minds for an intuitive understanding and answer, only a teacher can determine if we have reached this deep understanding. It can be an exhilarating, frustrating, bewildering and rewarding practice, and it has profoundly deepened my practice. If you want to work on koans, find a Zen Buddhist teacher to help you.

The Nature of Prayer

In my own journey, I was puzzled about how to pray. Obviously there were prayers that could be said, either of my own invention or from the liturgy, but my question was *how* does one pray.

I asked Mary Strouse, a practicing Catholic, how she explains how prayers have become meaningful for her: "Part of the meaning comes from *listening* to the prayer you're reciting"; by listening to the prayer, over time we can understand it and learn from it. When asked about prayer, Dr. Muzzamil Siddiqi explained it this way: "The Prophet [Muhammad] says you pray to God as if you're seeing Him, even though you see Him not, but He sees you; this is the experience one should have. So when you pray, you should not make an image of Him, but still you have to feel He is hearing you, He's in front of you, and you are talking to Him. It is said when you start your prayers, God turns His face toward you, and you pray as if you are talking to Him."

Meditation and Prayer

Centering prayer comes out of the Catholic tradition. Kay Lindahl described it to me this way: "With centering prayer, I spend 20 minutes twice a day in silence. The intention is to be present with the spirit, the source, whatever one calls it. You start out by choosing a sacred word or love word, so when you are meditating and become aware of anything, you go to that word to get you present again, so you don't follow your thoughts down the path that they take you. I love the practice, it's like brushing my teeth, and I miss it when I don't do it; I don't always feel like doing it and I do it anyway, because I know the fruits and it's made an amazing difference in my life." You can select any word, such as love or peace or God, but choose a word that is special for you, and hold that word in your heart as you sit and meditate.

Ignatian prayer was mentioned by a number of people. Karen Goran, a spiritual director in Anaheim, California, describes it this way: "The Ignatian way of praying the scriptures is visualization, of reading the scripture and meditating with it in terms of seeing it play out in the mind's eye, and to be different characters in each story. So if there are several people in that story, you can be all the different people, even be God or Jesus."

Science of Mind provides a format for meditative prayer; the Reverend Margie Clark of the Church of Religious Science in Seal Beach, California, describes the process this way:

> When praying you acknowledge that you already have everything, you only have to accept it. So in prayer we declare "what is" at a higher level. There are five steps: (1) The first step is recognition, where we acknowledge that God "is" and we declare whatever that is for us—"God is everything," "Spirit is life," "Divine energy is love." (2) The second step, we unify with that, so we say, "I am one with God, and since I am one with God, I am love, joy, beauty. . ." I express that God in me, as me, is me. (3) The realization step is to declare what is, we pray for specifics—material or spiritual. For example, "Today I declare that my life is good, I experience and know infinite abundance, my body is healthy and it has an intelligence to know how to correct itself, and anything that's out of order in my body is corrected. I experience abundance and health today." (4) The fourth step is thanksgiving—so we give thanks for what already is—"I give thanks for all the good in my life; for a healthy body that is beautiful and works well; it does that without any help from me, and it knows how to take care of itself and be a perfect instrument for me to use. I am thankful, knowing the truth is being manifest in my life right now." (5) The last step is release—"I release this into the law of mind, and let God/Power do its work, knowing that it is already done." Some people will say they want to pray because they feel sick, and I say "Don't pray with sickness in mind, what is it that you want?" That way they have to make the transition from feeling sick to feeling how it is to be well; I ask, "How do you want to feel, can you picture it if you were without the discomfort that you're in right now," so that their minds shift. It's like the sore toe, if my toe hurts, all I think about is the toe, and I forget the rest of my body is functioning beautifully. Our basic

belief is that where you put your energy and your thought, that is what will expand in your experience.

Pastor Preston Price had these thoughts on prayer:

If I'm talking to somebody, I'll say, "let me give you a gift. Here's a way to pray that you can pray all the time; it's ancient and yet your personal prayer." I'll say, "Give me your favorite name for God," and he or she says "I like Lord" or "I like praying to Jesus, or Father." Then I ask, "What is it you most want from God"—sometimes it'll be specific and the person may say, "I want to get rid of this pain," and I'll ask what's underneath that, sometimes it's peace, or understanding the world, so the person might say "Grant me understanding, or, let me see, show me the way, yeah, that's it, show me the way." So then I may ask about a name for God again—"How about Divine Wisdom," and they'll say, "No, that's too academic, I see God as more personal." So I'll say, "How about friend Jesus?"—and if they agree, they've created a breath prayer—"Friend Jesus, show me the way." Then as you take a breath in, you pray "Friend Jesus," and pray "show me the way' as you exhale. And so as you exhale and let go, you're asking to be shown, and as you inhale, you're taking in the Spirit and naming it."

I explained to Father John McAndrew that many of us have difficulty figuring out how to pray. He responded,

I've said the same thing: I don't know how to pray. And in scripture, one of Paul's letters says, "we don't know how to pray as we ought," so God provides us a way to do that, by taking our groans and our moaning, and we raise that up to God. Sometimes that's the most authentic prayer. The inarticulate "aaaaaaaahhhhhhh," the expression of powerlessness, is a profound prayer. In AA I help folks expand their repertoire of prayer, out of this heady thing that is all about thinking and words and pictures, into the wider conscious contact with God, a physicality, a sense of closeness, a remembering; all of those are conscious contact with God. There are multitudinous ways of having conscious contact; don't limit yourself to a particular form.

Meditation and prayer can help us move our spirits through difficult times. Father Brad Karelius gives an example:

My son's illness has been such that things can change just like that; his seizures are not under control. We'll get a good period, and all of a sudden there'll be a crisis; he's had many times when he's almost died. I remember beginning this exercise when my son was going through a lot of illness again. So I began by taking scripture, maybe just a few words, repeating them, and always inviting Jesus into my midst and asking the Lord to be present. I would meditate in my son's room; I'd usually meditate at night in the dark. I'd read the scriptures and sit in the room with the night-light, and he'd be in bed sleeping, and I'd be with him. Sometimes I'd lie on the floor and have a lot of desolate feelings; other times I'd meditate in the garden and found that energizing. It could be very hard, trying to quiet the mind, but I realized it was a practice I had to keep working at. Sometimes, after meditating, I would wash dishes and then write in my journal, which was like writing to God. Out of this, some things began to happen, some movement. Meditation is more than relaxation exercises.

Practice in Everyday Life

The way we live our daily lives from one moment to the next can be a spiritual practice. For me, everyday practice is *not* a substitute for a daily meditative or prayer practice; before I took this path, my everyday experience was dominated by busyness, responding to life in reactive and unconscious ways, and a preoccupation with wishing life were different. Everyday life now gives me the opportunity to manifest the unconscious or subconscious maturation that my contemplative or meditative practices have provided; I've become more conscious and aware, and notice that I have more choices about how I want to respond to life.

If we don't take our practice into our everyday life, we are missing perhaps the most important part of spiritual existence. Swami Atmavidyananda of the Vedanta Society of Southern California shared with me, "We can always try to practice keeping focused on our task and controlling the thoughts of the mind so that it's not distracted, which helps to strengthen the mind. We can also try to do our work with the attitude of total concentration and do it as an offering to God, and then also be detached from the results. You try to do as good a job as you can because you're offering it to God, but no matter how it comes out, you offer it, good or bad, and then don't worry about it; you don't get all excited because it was great, and you don't get depressed because it was bad." Every moment provides a wealth of spiritual seeds for our own growth. We simply have to plant them, nurture them and harvest their fruits in our daily lives.

There are simple practices where we can make daily life a spiritual practice. Eating can be a contemplative practice; so often we're busy talking or reading something and before we know it, we can't remember finishing our meal. Instead, you can express your gratitude for the food on your plate, and then notice the colors and textures of the food, experience the movement of using your fork, or cutting with a knife and how the utensils feel in your hands; tasting the food and noticing the smell of it; simply becoming one with the experience of the act which fundamentally sustains our lives. Washing dishes can be a meditative experience: giving thanks for the water, experiencing the water's heat, the texture, color and smell of the soap, the clanging of the pots and pans, the expansion and contraction of a sponge in your hand. One of the most meaningful spiritual experiences of daily life can be the practice of simply listening to another: being fully present, listening without judgment, opening your heart, withholding advice—all of these can be spiritual practices that enrich our lives.—

My consulting work offers many opportunities for practicing my spiritual life. When I have an individual who is disruptive or resistant in a training program, how can I work with that? How can I come from a place of compassion and not aggression? How can I empathize instead of criticize? How can I allow the person to have his or her feelings and ensure that the training experience for everyone else is productive and one of integrity?

I see my relationship with my husband as a spiritual practice. A couple of years ago he was unhappy in corporate America, and I encouraged him to become an independent consultant, even though I knew it might create some financial insecurity for us and he would be gone a great deal of the time. (And I happen to like having him around!) He took that step and has loved serving clients precisely as he chooses to serve them. Each day he is gone, I think of how I can transmit my love and caring to him, and when he is home, I think of all the little ways I can do the same. How do I practice when missing him? How do I fully experience the full range of emotions when I send him off for weeks, and how do I adjust to his being home? All these are questions that, when seen as spiritual practice, offer me the opportunity to open my heart to relationship and love.

In their book, *Gifts of the Spirit, Living the Wisdom of the Great Religious Traditions*, Philip Zaleski and Paul Kaufman talk about how the mundane can take on special significance:

> It's difficult to find much spiritual significance in washing our ears, brushing our teeth, or sitting on the toilet bowl. Yet many religions see the need to bring these earthy activities under the auspices of the inner life. Indeed, since we usually wash and dress, shave or put on makeup, in a fog, mulling over today's chores or yesterday's romantic encounter, these morning procedures cry out for attention. Their very intimacy gives them a special value: for if I don't treat my own body and its daily functions with respect, how will I treat the body of other human beings (not to mention their souls) and the body of the world?[2]

Sister Jane DeLisle suggests looking at how you see God in everyday circumstances, becoming a person of discernment, which is a lifelong practice:

> How did I live my life today conscious of God's presence, how has God been with me? In context I may not notice it, but in reflecting on it, how was God in that experience with me? At times I've fought that experience, and sometimes I went with it, reflecting on encounters with people during the day. It enables you to reflect on how you've been with God during the day and how you have lived life in the manner of Jesus and lived the values you say you believe in . . . where was God really powerful and where did I feel God's presence, where did I ignore God and went my own way and made a mess of things, or how could it have been different? You pay attention to your feelings all day long—what buttons got pushed—and ask for God's grace.

---

2. Philip Zaleski and Paul Kaufman, *Gifts of the Spirit: Living the Wisdom of the Great Religious Traditions* (San Francisco: HarperSanFrancisco, 1997), p.38.

Practicing the presence of God is another ancient practice. Pastor Craig Lockwood shares his understanding of this practice: "Practicing the presence of God is practicing the moment-to-moment awareness that God is with me. I have a book by a monk [the Brother Lawrence of the Resurrection, the 17th century Catholic monk and cook], and he is known for his practice of the presence of God, so even though he had a simple job, he wanted in his heart purpose to be constantly aware of the presence of God and of God's will in that moment, so he was pressing into his awareness of God and his obedience to him, and as a result he had this incredible joy that was really contagious."

Pastor Van Pewthers talks about God in everyday life: "It's sort of that ongoing sense of asking God into everything I do, so whether it's a business decision or a family decision or any kind of aspect of what I'm doing, I don't become paralyzed and not do, but I tell God that I want Your heart, Your mind, Your spirit to be part of the things I'm doing right now, so help me to make good decisions. Even more than that, be part of the decision making process with me, and if I'm doing the wrong thing, I want to be open to Your input; I'm going to believe that You love me enough that if I step out to do something, if it's not what You want, You'll change the way I step."

Practice in everyday life can also include volunteerism. Nicolee Jikyo Miller McMahon Sensei of the Three Treasures Zen Community, Vista, California spoke of the importance of volunteerism. "I actually feel that volunteerism is very important to any spiritual tradition, to any religious tradition. It's a spiritual practice to give of one's time and energy to help something develop and create a container for others, so it develops a sense of 'it's not just me, there are others,' they're the unseen others, they're the others who have come or the ones who have yet to come. To volunteer is a very profound practice, and I frankly would call it a spiritual practice."

Jikyo Sensei also spoke to the importance of integrating the spiritual life with the rest of daily life. "I also feel it's a valuable spiritual practice to really work with integrating one's every day life and family with spiritual practice; for example, one does a kind of plunging, a kind of deep practice in *sesshin* (retreat), and to not integrate that as one's life, and to confuse that monastic or *sesshin* environment as what I should be doing, and believing that my everyday life is secondary to me, is a great loss."

Bishop Murray Finck explains how he uses his practice in everyday life: "I was thinking about how I was going to have a long drive to a meeting the next day, a four-hour meeting that I didn't have much interest in, but needed to be there because of my position. Then I would have that long drive back home during rush hour traffic. I wasn't too excited about the meeting. The next morning the word 'opportunity' rose up during my prayers as my theme for the day. When I got in my car, I focused on the long drive as an opportunity. Instead of lamenting the day and the drive, I contemplated on my opportunities throughout the day."

Rabbi Steve Robbins also spoke of the importance of taking our meditation into the world: "In Judaism, there is nothing that is not meditative, so that my sitting here and speaking with you is as much a meditative experience as my quiet moments of solitude in meditative prayer, and they have just the same force and impact. In fact, to leave it all in those moments of solitude is a shame, because it is only when it comes out into the world in action, that it makes sense at all."

Sister Jane told me a story about relating to our spirit in every day life:

> A group of scientists were studying an aboriginal people in the desert. And the nomad people would trek and trek, and then they'd turn around and face the direction they'd just left; and they'd wait. Then they'd turn around and walk for a long time in a single row, and go to the next place, and they'd stop, turn around and look and wait, and the scientists were all arguing about what this behavior meant. So one of them decided to ask the leader of the nomad people, "Why do you walk and stop and look and then walk—why don't you keep going?" And the nomad answered, "We are a people who are very busy; we're about moving and about our journey and about getting to our next location, but every now and then we need to stop and look where we've been and allow our spirits to catch up. . ."

Where to Go From Here

You might be feeling just a little overwhelmed at this point, depending on how far along you are on your spiritual path. In Chapter 10 you will find a more in-depth description of potential next steps. But let me make some suggestions so that you don't leave this chapter discouraged or perplexed. My suggestions are divided according to some arbitrary divisions of where you might be on your own spiritual journey: (1) If you are participating in a religious community but do not have a personal practice; (2) If you have an individual spiritual practice but do not participate in a religious community; (3) If you are not participating in a religious community and also do not have a personal practice.

If You are Practicing in a Religious Community Without a Personal Practice . . .

There are a few steps you might consider taking if you are already affiliated with a religious community and feel that your participation in that community meets your communal needs:

- Practice some of the meditation and prayer activities described in this chapter on your own. Be sure to give yourself at least a couple of weeks to try out each practice, and don't try more than one or two at a time. Keep it simple.
- Ask the spiritual leader of your religious organization if he or she is a trained spiritual director or has training in meditation or developing personal prayer practices. Read Chapter 7 for suggestions regarding the selection of a spiritual teacher. If your congregation's spiritual leader does not do this type of training, perhaps he or she can refer you to someone who does.
- Check other sources for meditation training. (See Chapter 10 for specific information.)

Whatever you do, don't give up. The spiritual path sometimes presents obstacles, and they are worth overcoming if you truly have the call or desire to deepen your connection to the Infinite One.

If You Have an Individual Spiritual Practice But Do Not Practice in Religious Community . . .

Finding a religious community can be viewed as a spiritual trek. I am thinking of the story of how there is a mountain, and the mountain is very high, and the top of the mountain is being with God. But because the mountain is so high and large it encompasses a variety of climates and types of terrain. On the mountain are various people who have figured out different paths to climb to the top of the mountain. They wear different types of clothing, follow different methods of climbing. They share the same goal, but are approaching the task of climbing to the summit, to being with God, in different ways.

If you see the exploration of religious community as a mountain trek, you will find this exploration to be intriguing and rewarding.

- If you were raised in a religion and are not averse to investigating it, find a congregation in your area.
- If you want to start fresh, read about different religions, or ask friends which communities they participate in, and why they appreciate their religion and its community; you might want to attend with them. (It might be helpful to let them know you're just exploring.) A critical factor to keep in mind is that spiritual trek will take time, preparation and patience; you have to do your homework before you embark. And once you're trekking, you have to be prepared for the unexpected; it goes with the territory.
- Keep in mind that the religion and the community need to be treated as separate research projects: you might be drawn to a religion, but you don't feel comfortable with the personality of a particular community. Or you might enjoy the people, but the religion doesn't speak to you. Once you find the religion that meets your moral, ethical, and spiritual needs, then take time to find the community that complements it.

If You are Not Part of a Religious Community and Do Not Have a Personal Practice . . .

This is tricky. Where to start? You can take a couple of tacks:

- If the idea of religious community calls to you, start your research right away; you might find support for developing a personal practice along the way.
- If you're uncomfortable about participating in religious community, then start with a spiritual practice; there may be nondenominational meditation groups in your community, too, that will support this first step; check with churches, Zen centers or synagogues in your area.

The critical point is to take action. Spirit is summoning you to nourish your soul space and to let down the barriers you have been experiencing between you and the One. If you pursue this path, even with its inherent difficulties and challenges, and having to face "not-knowing," you will not regret it.

CHAPTER FIVE

What Kind of Commitment Does It Take?

... the fact is that anyone who has used the moments and days and years of his or her life to become wiser, kinder, and more at home in the world has learned from what has happened right now. We can aspire to be kind right in the moment, to relax and open our heart and mind to what is in front of us right in the moment. Now is the time. If there's any possibility for enlightenment, it's right now, not at some future time. Now is the time. ~ PEMA CHODRON, *When Things Fall Apart*

Today is the day I volunteer at the hospital. Sometimes I become preoccupied with learning how to fill the nurses' refrigerators, or marking the fluid intake of a patient, or trying to remember which utility room has the good ice machine. But today I was reminded why I come here.

Two ladies were my "teachers" today and touched my heart. One, Mrs. D., was so frightened when I saw her the week before; she was sure they were moving her from her room because they thought she was going to die. I watched an experienced patient services volunteer try to reassure her, but there was nothing she could say to lessen her fear. I simply watched, feeling helpless and uncomfortable that I had nothing to offer to comfort her. Today I saw Mrs. D again. When I walked by her room, she caught my eye, and she was smiling! I chatted with her, telling her how nice it was to see her. After I left her room, I couldn't help but think how all of us experience the ever-changing nature of our lives in such different ways, depending on our circumstances, our mindset, and our health.

Then there was Mrs. K. She's been in the hospital for weeks, and I usually see her daughter, and often her son-in-law, visiting with her. Her daughter seems so sweet—she must be at least in her 60s or 70s, since Mrs. K is 96. Mrs. K had lived in her own home alone until recently, and suddenly her life had turned a corner, and she wasn't keeping up. She was clearly agitated that afternoon and her daughter was not in at that time. I walked by and I could see and hear her talking to herself, shaking her head from one side to the other. When I walked in, she was trying to explain her physical state, frustrated and alarmed at the same time. I decided to talk with a nurse, who acknowledged Mrs. K's agitation, and explained that there was nothing anyone could do. I returned to her room, and struggled with how I could simply witness her pain and anxiety and simply be present for her without feeling compelled to "do something," since there was probably nothing that could be done. I knew that trying to talk her out of her fear and loneliness was not going to be helpful. As she continued to talk with me, I started to reflect her feelings back to her—"You're scared because you don't understand what's happening to you right now. . . you're frustrated because no one seems to be able to help . . ." and she would acknowledge what I was saying. I just stayed there with her, and we exchanged thoughts and feelings—and suddenly she smiled. I don't know what either of us had said just before, but she smiled. I smiled in return. She lifted her right hand slightly, smiled again and said, "thank you so much." I felt my own tears of gratitude, because at another time I would have left the room at the onset of my anxiety, rather than simply being present to whatever came up. Instead I realized that I didn't have to do anything; I only had to be with her and be a witness to, and honor, Mrs. K and her fear.

Part of my Zen practice is to commit myself, even in difficult situations, to experience moments of genuine, heartfelt connection, without having to alter what is simply present. Although I am half the age of Mrs. K, I live with my own fears, my own frustrations, my own feelings of helplessness, bewilderment, and loneliness. I was grateful that we made that emotional/spiritual connection, and that instead of trying to make her emotional pain go away, I could commit to stay with her, be attentive to her, and relate to what she was experiencing.

Commitment to spiritual practice asks us to be willing to face pain and fear, in ourselves and in others. We can choose to run away from these frightening situations; we can try to find ways to understand and deal with them intellectually; however, sometimes the rational mind can prevent us from making a spiritual connection. The rational mind should not be discarded in assessing the path we take, but a life of spirit is much more expansive than our analytical mind can ever fully comprehend. It is the rational mind *and* the intuitive mind, it is the intellect *and* the compassionate heart, it is the moral compass *and* the forgiving spirit, it is the practical *and* the incomprehensible, that will illuminate our spiritual path.

We don't need to be worried about commitment in spiritual practice when things are going well. When we pray or meditate and we are filled with Spirit and at peace, we look forward to the time we set aside for our spiritual lives. But much of spiritual practice can be mundane or ordinary or boring. It can seem too time consuming or demanding when we have other things we prefer to do, activities that are certain to make us feel good, if only temporarily. The rewards of the spiritual life, however, come from spending dedicated time with Spirit over time, whether we are always moved to do it—or not. (This concept will be discussed further in Chapter 9.)

In this chapter, I will describe the kind of commitment that a deep spiritual practice requires: the importance of *showing up*; the *willingness to take risks;* and *faith*. The more you nurture your practice in these ways, the more you are likely to experience the profundity and meaning of a rich spiritual life.

Showing Up

One foundational aspect of spiritual practice is quite simple: show up. Regardless of how we feel, or what we'd rather be doing, we need to make time to pray, meditate or be with other spiritual friends. Making a commitment to honor Spirit by picking a particular time of the day to practice communing with the Divine or opening up to the present moment—that's showing up.

What is Commitment and Discipline?

Most of us relish our freedom and independence; the United States was founded on the values of these concepts. Unfortunately freedom and independence have come to mean something completely different than they were intended to mean. In the early 21st century, we've come to believe that to maintain our freedom, we have to abandon commitment and discipline. We think that committing to an idea, an activity or goal limits our freedom and our enjoyment of life. When we commit, we believe that we miss out on having fun, doing whatever we want, and being spontaneous. Realistically we know that having a fun and interesting life all the time is not possible, and yet if we are honest with ourselves, we realize our lives are dominated by this desire.

The key to leading a rich life from the perspective of valuing commitment and discipline is to recognize what they offer us, instead of what we might be giving up. For example, if I commit to going to my Zen community every Tuesday night, I will give up one evening with my husband, a favorite television show, or an opportunity to curl up with a good book; however, I will also have the opportunity to have an extended period to sit or meditate, a chance to interview with my teacher, and time to visit with spiritual friends and to be available for them. From a universal perspective, I am putting aside precious time to connect with the infinite, to relate to that which is Spirit. When I weigh the benefits against the losses, the choice is relatively easy for me to make.

Commitment is only half the goal; intention is not enough. I need to practice discipline by actually going to my Zen community even though I may not feel like going; when I'm feeling grumpy; when I'm tired. My experience, almost without exception, is that every time I attend when I don't feel like it, I am grateful afterwards that I went. Often my spirits are raised and I feel gratified and fulfilled by sharing spirit time with others.

Rabbi Steve Robbins describes the importance of discipline in this way: "Discipline is probably the most complex and difficult of human skills to learn, so that spirituality, like all human talents, is a learned skill. It is the devotion to discipline that makes the difference." Kay Lindahl, Executive Director for the Alliance for Spiritual Community, talks about making time for personal spiritual practice: "The most important aspect of an individual spiritual practice is the discipline of it, doing it on a regular basis. I tell people when I teach centering prayer, you make an appointment with God and you keep it, regardless. I keep my appointment with the dentist because I know it's good for me, and I keep my appointment with God because it's part of my spiritual well-being."

The paradox of having discipline in spiritual practice is that it provides us with more, not less freedom, more, not fewer gifts. Because spiritual practice opens us up, we expand our awareness of life and appreciate it more than ever before; we are free to open ourselves to more experiences, are less fearful of what we may encounter, are more curious in our explorations of life, and find more joy in the simplest of occurrences.

By practicing spiritual discipline and showing up for spiritual time, we are able to face the turbulence and chaos of our lives with more equanimity, and allow for the ever-changing nature of every day existence. We learn to flow with the stream, to be more flexible and open to the possibilities of each unfolding moment. When I get extremely busy, it's easy for me to stress out, to become overwhelmed by the demands of my work. Although I still become overwhelmed at times, I have learned to reflect on my emotional state, and to understand that my thoughts about the busyness of my schedule, not necessarily the schedule itself, are creating my stress. By this simple acknowledgment, and the reminder to pace myself from one moment to the next, I not only find that my anxiety decreases dramatically, but I am more available to the people with whom I work, and I enjoy my work much more.

How Much Must I Do?

When I asked Rabbi Jonathan Omer-Man about the kind of commitment required to maintain a spiritual practice, he answered simply: "Daily." He continued by saying, "For me, I think it's important to understand that a practice is a process, not an event. You can't do it once a week or in a once-a-year retreat. It's a daily practice. That doesn't mean you don't have a crisis where you don't do it for six weeks, but ultimately it's a daily process."

Spiritual practice has a cumulative effect on our lives. There isn't a formula for determining the amount of time you should devote to a spiritual practice each day, or even the number of times per day. More important than the amount of time is your establishing a regular practice that you follow every day.

I found it extremely difficult to sit still, when I first started to meditate. Five minutes felt like five hours. For a couple of months I meditated in the evenings for ten minutes, then gradually increased that amount to 15, then 20 minutes. I stayed at 20 minutes for several more months, and finally felt ready to commit to 30 minutes per sitting period. After four years, I felt I wanted to not only have a Zen sitting practice in the evening, but I wanted to have a Jewish prayer practice, too. So after several years of resisting the idea of sitting twice a day, suddenly the decision seemed to be the most natural thing in the world. Where I set a quiet timer to announce the end of my sitting period in the evening, I do Jewish meditation until I "feel I'm finished" in the morning; this period usually lasts 15 to 30 minutes. I'm not sure why I like having less structure for my morning prayer and meditation, but it feels appropriate, and I like the flexibility. Once I finish morning meditation, I often write in my journal.

If you're just beginning a daily practice, be conservative about the amount of time you dedicate to a personal spiritual practice, and then stick with it, unless or until you feel ready to increase the length of time. Also pick a type of practice that you are willing to do daily for one month; any practice you try will probably feel awkward or strange or uncomfortable, if you've never done it before, so you'll need adjustment time. Only time will tell you whether a practice will work for you or not. If after a month you find that a practice does not suit you, try something else. Sometimes, too, a practice that is uncomfortable for you at one point in your spiritual life will suit you perfectly at another time.

That's what "showing up" is all about: making a promise to yourself to engage in spiritual time every day, and following through on your commitment. The regular, consistent pledge to practice is the foundation of a strong spiritual life.

Willingness to Take Risks

Engaging in a spiritual practice is a risky business. Although it can bring great beauty, spiritual understanding and peace into one's life, it can also cause pain and confusion. On balance, most of us who pursue a dedicated spiritual life would probably say that the benefits far outweigh the losses; that moments of being filled with God's love and evolving in our own personal development enrich our lives far more than the difficult periods trouble us. In committing to a spiritual life, we need to embrace all of existence, which means allowing ourselves to be vulnerable, and being willing to face the darkness and difficult times.

Being Vulnerable

It's Monday night, and I am sitting with a group at sensei's house. Ordinarily I don't attend on Monday nights, but I hadn't seen my teacher in a while, and was really struggling with the koan, "Kyogen's Man Up A Tree." I figured I could explain to her why my conflict with the koan demonstrated that koan practice wasn't working for me, and it would justify my discontinuing it, particularly since I'd been working with this koan for months and the frustration of resolving this particular section was disturbing my spiritual peace of mind

As I sat down for my interview with sensei, I began to explain why I wanted to end my work on koans. I'm such a hard worker in other aspects of my practice that I was sure she'd let me off the hook. But she didn't. I was stunned, then angry at her response. She told me that she would not be serving me well as my teacher if she didn't hold me to the task. I lamented that I would never finish koan practice in this lifetime, at this rate. She reminded me that one of the great Zen masters didn't finish koan practice until his '70s. She said she knew I could do the work. That the koan was pointing out my stuck places. That she had more faith in me than I had in myself. I sat there, frustrated and angry, the tears falling down my cheeks, my head downcast with remorse that I had ever asked to work on koans. She concluded the interview, and I picked up my sitting pillow and cut short my sitting with the rest of the group. As I drove home, I seesawed between anger and grief, disappointment and frustration.

When I finally arrived home, I realized she was right. I couldn't give up now. She'd even told me that once I resolved this koan, I could decide whether I wanted to continue koan practice or work on another type of practice. But first I had to complete this task. Jikyo Sensei had never sent me an e-mail regarding my practice; all our discussions were in interview. But the next morning I was deeply touched by a note she sent me written later the previous night: "Dear Jyokai, the sacred is your pain, your frustration. You can see into this knotted koan—you can do it. After that we can forget koan study. I trust you."

The next night, Tuesday night, was the night I usually went to sit at the Zen center, and I figured I'd simply not sign up for interview that night, since I was still feeling vulnerable and over-whelmed, in spite of my resolve to continue working on the koan. But sensei asked her attendant to bring me in anyway. As soon as I finished my bows and sat down, I began to cry again. I told her that I knew she was right, that I was giving up on myself and that somehow the koan reflected places where I was stuck in my own life, and that I would continue to work on it. In a gentle and reassuring tone, she emphasized that I could resolve the koan, and that she would be there for me.

Two weeks later, I finished my work on the koan. The answer, as often happens, was obvious. I refused to see it, because it reflected *my own fears about simply letting go. So often in life I have held on tightly to so many things: my ideas, my decisions, my opinions, being right, looking good. The koan had become my teacher, and I recognized its lesson and its truth, in both my heart and mind, and in my own life.*

The spiritual journey nurtures our ability to open to each unfolding moment and every aspect of our lives. Opening in this way, we begin to allow ourselves to be vulnerable; as we open our hearts to the infinite and inexplicable, we open ourselves to possibility. And the possibilities can include great satisfaction and fulfillment, and they can also provide great sorrow and frustration. Nicolee Jikyo Miller-McMahon Sensei describes vulnerability in this way:

> I think a spiritual practice requires a deep commitment to one's self, and if you're working with a teacher or rabbi or priest, it requires a commitment to be honest, trustworthy and accountable. In the Zen tradition it requires a willingness to face and see things that one doesn't want to face and a willingness to open the heart-mind. To me, it's a real commitment to letting go of looking good and being right, which is what drives most people and doesn't allow them to deepen their practice, because they're more committed to being right or more committed to making an impression, rather than being honest and revealing themselves.

As our spiritual life deepens, we begin to see more clearly who we are, and how we create barriers between ourselves and the rest of the world. We observe our own thoughts, actions and behaviors dispassionately, and begin to recognize our self-centeredness and separateness that have always been there, but have been hidden from us. As we begin to notice our desires and efforts to get our children in the best schools, to buy ourselves nice clothes, to have glamorous bodies, to buy the latest car, and to get the next promotion, we realize the colossal efforts we make to distinguish ourselves from everybody else. We realize that underneath our actions to take care of ourselves and others is an insatiable ego wanting to be protected, recognized and fed. Our energies are focused on getting enough stuff to insulate ourselves from the vagaries and painfulness of our lives.

The beauty of spiritual practice is that we may decide to continue these self-gratifying efforts, but we begin to better understand what we are doing. We become a witness to not only our conduct, but to our motivation: the desire to acquire enough money, material things and status, in order to feel comfortable, satisfied and safe. Sometimes these motivations are so deeply buried in our psyches that, until our practices deepen, we aren't able to identify their origins or understand their nature.

When we recognize that we cannot make ourselves perpetually comfortable or invulnerable, we may begin to rebel. We'll explain all the actions we *can* take to save ourselves. But those efforts are illusions, too. As long as we are alive, we are vulnerable, susceptible to our own emotions, to human whims and natural disasters. When we begin to realize these truths not only in our heads, but in our hearts, our wounds from being in the world begin to heal. Our healing comes from our opening up our lives, because we not only open to others, but we allow God to fill the places where we hurt. We realize the Divine in ourselves, the part of us that surrenders to the inevitable, to truth, to integrity, to that which simply is. And as our hurts fill with Spirit, and we heal, we feel our hearts expand just a little more, and that too allows Spirit to enter and mend us once again. It's as natural as breathing, in and out, opening and closing, hurting and healing, submitting to the everyday and encountering the One.

The Darkness

When we engage in a spiritual practice, we make ourselves available to the Light. But to fully experience the radiance of Spirit, we must also be willing to investigate and face our own darkness. As the Rev. Kikanza Nuri Robins states, "An effective spiritual practice requires a willingness to go places you haven't been before, and a willingness to experience yourself differently." We might be motivated to pursue a spiritual journey because we are looking only for light, only for joy, only for satisfaction. But the true spiritual journey means embracing all of life: the light and the darkness, the sadness and the joy, the disappointments and the satisfaction. This is what Sister Jane DeLisle says about the difficult times:

> When you engage in a spiritual practice and it feels good, you hang in there. But when you hit the rocky parts, it's not the time to quit. Teresa of Avila said most people make it to the 'third mansion of' the inner life and then quit, because it gets too hard, because that fourth place is that transformative place of moving from what I do, to letting God do it in me. So part of the discipline is to move through fears and not avoid them; it's a matter of attending to your inner self and noticing what you need to pay attention to, then getting the help of a friend, therapist, spiritual director—someone who's wiser on the journey.

I think, compared to some people, my struggles have been few. Since, at the date of this writing, I have been practicing for six years, my personal development has been more gradual than dramatic. I've not had great periods or events of either light or darkness, of the dramatic or the sublime. My transformation is an evolving one, and my expectations are simple. Although at times I acknowledge a desire for some kind of profound "opening" experience, most of the time I am satisfied with the day-to-day realizations about my life and how I relate to the universe. At times I have been miserable when I finally realize how I have burdened myself with my desires and delusions about life, and struggled periodically with truths I did not want to see. But for the most part, my spiritual practice has been steady and true. Those who know me well might say that I underrate the impact of, and my willingness to deal with the difficulties of my life, that I have struggled and faced darkness more than I acknowledge. Regardless, I am willing to face the light and darkness, because there is no way to pursue this path without being willing to face both.

Part of this spiritual darkness is hidden in our shadow. Jungian psychology describes the shadow as those parts of us that we find unacceptable and have learned to deny and repress in ourselves, beginning very early in life. Shadow is often described as the dark or evil sides of ourselves, but it also includes attributes that we deem negative or unattractive. We can also have a shadow that includes positive attributes that we were told were unacceptable and therefore we were not willing to acknowledge them within ourselves.

Because our shadow sides are buried in our subconscious, we are not aware of these characteristics and therefore do not recognize them in ourselves. Robert Bly describes the shadow in our lives in this way:

> When we were one or two years old we had what we might visualize as a 360-degree personality. Energy radiated out from all parts of our body and all parts of our psyche. A child running is a living globe of energy. We had a ball of energy, all right; but one day we noticed that our parents didn't like certain parts of that ball. They said things like: 'Can't you be still?' Or 'It isn't nice to try and kill your brother.' Behind us we have an invisible bag, and the part of us our parents don't like, we, to keep our parents' love, put in the bag.[1]

The older we get, the fuller our shadow bag becomes. We get a glimpse of our shadow when we see it in other people; as others act out the attributes that we were told were forbidden, we often become outraged to see others demonstrating those behaviors, which, at a subconscious level, we have buried and have labeled unacceptable.

As we pursue a spiritual practice, our shadows often begin to emerge. The shadow bag that has held our darkest secrets begins to slowly open, as the bindings that we've used to seal it become unraveled. The depths of the subconscious begin to surface. At first we only see our shadows reflected more and more in the actions of others; we're repulsed at the "unforgivable misbehaviors" of those around us. But as our spiritual practices develop, we begin to realize, on our own and with the help of others, that the actions and behaviors of people that appall, disappoint and enrage us are simply mirrors of our own denied selves. We feel the pain, the embarrassment and confusion of those aspects that we believe have never been part of us, and begin to recognize the distortions about who we are that have colored our perceptions.

---

1. Robert Bly, "The Long Bag We Drag Behind Us." in Connie Zweig and Jeremiah Abrams, (eds.) *Meeting the Shadow: The Hidden Power of the Dark Side of Human Nature* (New York: Tarcher, 1991), p.6.

As we recognize that these behaviors are only the distortions of who we are, we realize that we are not looking at another person, but we are truly looking at ourselves. And although integrating our shadow into our conscious psyche, learning to love all that we are, can be disorienting and painful, it is also wonderfully liberating. For through this uncomfortable and trying process, we become free to understand and embrace ourselves and everything that we are—and that is when we genuinely invite God into our lives. Instead of our energy being dedicated to erecting and maintaining barriers and images of who we are, we become more truly who we are, flawed and perfect, human and Divine.

Faith

So how do we get through the difficult times, the discouraging times, of spiritual practice? We need faith: faith that we are never alone, that we are never separate from God, and faith that on the other side of desperation and desolation are hope, reconciliation and peace. We can understand how faith manifests and is maintained through an understanding of the role of aspiration, by holding fast through the desert times, and by practicing perseverance.

Aspiration

In Zen Buddhism, we often talk about how desires create suffering. In my Zen community, we have replaced the word "desires" (often the translation used) with the word "delusions" in a line of the frequently chanted "Four Vows": "Delusions are inexhaustible; I vow to put an end to them." The reason we use the word *delusions* instead of *desires*, is because we *delude* ourselves into thinking that life should be a certain way, rather than embracing just what life offers. *Desire*, however, more closely resembles aspiration, the hopes and dreams and energy we have for moving along the spiritual path, regardless of the obstacles.

Aspiration is the desire that cuts through all the resistance we have to spiritual practice. It is the motivation that moves us to want to experience the Divine, to understand the meaning of life, to discover why we are here and how we can contribute. It is that which fuels our beliefs in the value of blasting away barriers and finding intimacy with all that exists. It comforts us at those moments when commitment falters, hope trembles and fear persists; it reenergizes us to hold steady, battle the storms of doubt and stay focused. We cannot manufacture aspiration; it must come from deep within. We must nurture it through our willingness to face the unknown and look darkness in the eye. At times our aspiration for spiritual practice may change; our goals may change, our priorities will shift, our practices will mature and move in a different direction. But the energy which desires to know that which can't be known, to understand that which cannot be understood, will persist and hold us to our vision.

The Desert Times

One of the most difficult periods of spiritual practice are those times when we feel that no matter how much time we spend in prayer, contemplation, or meditation, we feel distant from the universe and isolated from God. These times are referred to as the "desert times," or "dark times," or the "dark night of the soul." These periods of desolation can be short or very long, and their descriptions vary from person to person. Mary Strouse, a practicing Catholic describes the desert times in this way: "Sometimes it's like you're praying and you're just not getting your voice back. When you pray, it's like stepping through a door to God, but in the desert times, it's like you can't open the door—not that it's locked, but there's a screen. You're feeding in, but you don't feel anything coming back." Linda Klassen described the dark times metaphorically: "I drew a picture in my journal of a very rocky coastline, and there's a lighthouse up there. The whole scene is enshrouded with a very dense, wet, dark, foggy mist, and out there someplace, not too far from the rock, is a very small wooden boat; no sail, no oars, nothing; just me in the boat, by myself, without a coat, just simple clothing on, not knowing where I am, feeling the darkness and the cold and the wet. But every now and then there is a blip from that lighthouse, some gift is given. So I knew where I was and where I was supposed to be, whether I understood it or not."

For those who know the dark night of the soul, it is desolate and lonely. There are no tricks to ending it or overcoming it. Its arrival is always unforeseen, unpredictable and inexplicable. And its time of departure is impossible to know. But for those dedicated to practice, during the desert times, it seems impossible to abandon the path. Because deserting the path is the same as abandoning yourself. This is the point where one reaches into oneself and relies on discipline and commitment to get through the dark times and to ultimately re-engage with the Divine. So the emotional and spiritual risks exist. There is no avoiding them. But when we accept them, persevere in spite of them, we mature deeply into spirit and nurture our soul space.

Perseverance

"Teresa of Avila came up with this wonderful four-part metaphor about God's watering a garden and nourishing the virtues and the graces of our spirits," says the Rev. Lois McAfee. McAfee continues:

> First, as the bearers of these virtues that God has placed in us, we make a lot of effort, undertaking bible studies and other devotional disciplines, in order to enter into mutual prayer. The well containing God's water is far away, and we make great effort to haul our bucket to it. We drop the bucket in the well, lower it down, haul it up with great effort, and we get this little bit of water to water the flowers or virtues with. We get very little water doing this, but we keep at it until one day we realize that there is a hand pump nearby, so we take our bucket and put it under the pump. We prime the pump, again with our spiritual practices, and at first nothing comes out. Then suddenly water just pours out and our bucket is filled in no time flat. And even when we stop pumping, it keeps gushing: God's grace for us. There is more going on here than we can account for; we just showed up willingly with the bucket. From this we can water our virtues more and more, and this sense of growing more into the likeness of God begins to grow in us. One day we look within, in a period of dryness, and discover that underneath there is a hidden river that we can easily draw from. God is doing most of what is going on in us. Then comes the day when we wake up and it's raining and we're doing nothing and God is doing it all: sheer grace pouring onto our virtues in God's presence. That is what can happen to us, but it requires our faithfulness. That's why staying the course is so important.

Perseverance in faith means continually asking ourselves why we are on the spiritual path, and knowing that the answer must be given not just from the mind, but from the heart. Swami Sarvadevananda says, "At every opportunity I am to judge, 'Am I becoming more spiritual? Am I becoming more peaceful? Am I feeling the oneness in every person that I meet? Am I creating a new vision of the world?' Every day we should ask ourselves, is our faith leading us to God?"

Faith is not being afraid to ask ourselves the tough questions, because we know that the Divine, in some way, will answer; and faith is being willing to persist on the spiritual path, even when we can't hear the Divine answer. Faith is knowing that we may not hear the voice of God, but we will see God manifest in the opening of our hearts, in the voice of a child, in the glory of a beautiful spring day, in the hug of a friend. When we are most reluctant to listen because we feel alone or betrayed, faith reminds us that we are never alone, that betrayal and hurt are part of the journey, and that joy is accepting all of it as the wholeness, completeness of our lives.

Faith is not something that can be created; it is like a seed in our souls that manifests, and it must be nurtured and maintained. It is nurtured by our perseverance, our willingness to trudge the spiritual path when times are difficult, to celebrate our spiritual journeys when they are joyful, and to walk the path with openness and receptivity when life is simply ordinary. Even within ordinariness, Spirit is always present and available; we only need to be awake to Its omnipresent grace.

So a big part of spiritual practice is commitment: willingness to show up when we'd rather be somewhere else, willingness to take risks to open to both joy and pain, willingness to persevere when the path is filled with the brambles and boulders of life. The amount of commitment required cannot be measured, but neither can the profundity and rewards of leading a deeply spiritual life.

CHAPTER SIX

What is a Spiritual Teacher?

When I think of my own teacher I feel enormous gratitude continually, practically every moment of my life. It's gratitude that there was somebody who was brave enough and fierce enough and humorous enough and compassionate enough to get it through my thick skull that there's no place to hide. ~ PEMA CHODRON, *Start Where You Are*

For nearly a year and a half, I pursued my Zen practice on my own. I meditated nearly every day, felt the deepening of my practice almost from the first day I sat, and was moving along just fine. When I asked Zen teachers why they thought I ought to have a relationship with a teacher, their answers simply didn't seem to apply to me. I felt I was clear on my spiritual direction; I looked forward to my sitting practice, supplemented it with a periodic intensive retreat, and read up on Zen Buddhism.

Gradually, though, I realized something was missing. I had questions arise that I couldn't answer. Some of them were questions about Buddhism, other questions came up about the nature of my practice, and sometimes I was confused about whether my questions were about my practice, life itself, or both. For many months I weighed the pros and cons of working with a teacher: I knew I could learn more about deepening my practice; I could receive spiritual guidance when I didn't know where to look for answers; I could develop a relationship where my teacher could help me clarify my practice when I was confused, and would challenge and confront me when I required it, and comfort and reassure me when I needed that, too. But I also had concerns about selecting a teacher: how would I know if I had a good teacher? What would I do if we disagreed on how to pursue my spiritual path? How would I know if he or she were providing appropriate direction? How much independence would I have to sacrifice for the relationship? Until I could answer at least some of these questions, or have a teacher answer them, I continued to think that I must not be ready for a commitment to a teacher.

But I was wrong. I finally realized that some of my questions about the student-teacher relationship could only be answered by actually working with a teacher.

The time eventually came when I knew I needed to make a commitment to a teacher: I had progressed as far as I could on my own, and my stubborn determination to be independent was preventing me from exploring the benefits of an *interdependent* relationship with someone who could respect, teach and guide me. I had developed a casual relationship with a teacher whom I liked and admired, and decided to broach the topic. After we talked, I took more time to think over my commitment, and in a month's time, I asked him formally to be my teacher.

After working with that teacher long-distance for three years, I decided to work with a teacher closer to home. My current Zen teacher is Nicolee Jikyo Miller-McMahon, Sensei in Vista, California. She is a delight to work with; she is a marriage and family therapist by training, and some of those skills clearly help her in her work with students. I admire and appreciate her for her directness, intelligence, playfulness, commitment, humor and wisdom. We meet nearly every week to review my Zen practice. Although we haven't always agreed with each other, I've always felt that her guidance has come from a place of compassion and common sense. I see her as my spiritual friend, colleague, guide and mentor, and I will occasionally refer to my relationship with her in this chapter.

I also see Rabbi Jonathan Omer-Man as my teacher. Although my relationship with him is distant and sporadic, I trust him to give me wise and caring direction. My perception is that even if I had a more committed and involved relationship with Metivta, the center of which Rabbi Omer-Man is founder, my relationship with him would be less intimate than with my Zen teacher, due to my expectations and understanding of the typical rabbi-student relationship and our respective personalities. I treasure my connection with him, nonetheless.

So where are you in your practice? Just beginning? Searching and confused? Curious but unsure? Working with a teacher but looking for more? In this chapter I'll share my understanding of the role of the spiritual guide or teacher (the terms can be used interchangeably), and the student's role in relationship with him or her. I'll also discuss the reasons for seeking and selecting a spiritual guide or teacher; identify our informal spiritual teachers; describe the attributes of a formal spiritual teacher; explain the process of spiritual guidance; and offer suggestions for selecting a spiritual teacher.

Why Seek a Spiritual Teacher?

If you've never thought about having a spiritual teacher, this may seem foreign to you; you may have difficulty identifying with the need for finding a teacher and developing a student-teacher relationship. If you're having difficulty articulating your feelings about whether you might benefit from a spiritual teacher, the following thoughts might help.

- You have had a disappointing experience with religion or a religious leader in the past, and the scars still burn in your memory. You may still harbor resentment, fear or anger about your experiences. At the same time, you yearn to pursue a spiritual life, but don't know how to proceed on your own.

- You've been following a spiritual practice, but you feel like you're treading water. The practice has enriched your life, yet for a long time you've felt the need to stretch yourself, but you're not sure what to do. You may have even experimented with other religions or spiritual practices, and found them interesting for a while, but nothing seems to meet your spiritual needs.

- You've been attending church or services for a long time, and the communal experience can be uplifting and supportive, but you want to go deeper—you just aren't sure what that means. You feel the presence of God at times, but God is remote, distant. You crave an intimacy, an immediacy to your experience of the Divine, but you don't know how to go about achieving this relationship.

- You've had a terrible loss—a family member, friend or colleague has died. Or you've suffered some other type of loss that has left you desolate and angry. You wonder how God could allow these things to happen, and you've tried to make meaning of life without abandoning God, but it is a struggle. You need help in finding a way to get through your suffering and also in maintaining your relationship with God.

- This whole idea of spiritual direction is completely new to you. You've had little spirituality in your life, and you are clueless about how to find it or create it. You go to occasional retreats and workshops, but you don't know how or where to drive a stake in the ground, in order to make Spirit the center of your life.

A spiritual teacher is trained to deal with these kinds of issues; he or she can help you clarify what you are seeking, define the kind of practice that would suit your temperament, and determine the kind of commitment that will meet your needs. The teacher can also help you create a spiritual path that will help you heal from past experiences, by developing ways to live in the present moment and allow God into your life. Many spiritual directors even work with people from denominations other than their own, and welcome the opportunity to be available to others as they help them find ways to heal and move forward on their spiritual paths.

Who are Spiritual Teachers?

While the focus of this chapter is primarily on spiritual teachers with whom you have a formal and committed relationship, there are also "informal" teachers whom we may encounter when we least expect them. These are people who shift our perspectives and help us grow by asking tough spiritual questions or impart great wisdom in brief but significant encounters. Rabbi Jonathan Omer-Man says, "A person you meet on the San Diego-Los Angeles railroad who sits opposite you for 75 minutes could be your teacher and ask, 'Susan, where are you going?' Sometimes we encounter teachers in very, very short intensive encounters." Rabbi Omer-Man shared another tale of the unlikely teacher: "There's the story in the Bible with Abraham on his way west to Canaan, having a battle with ruffians, called 'kings' in the Bible. They were probably gang leaders, just like a guy with a Harley Davidson and 30 followers, who would be called the King of Sodom or the King of this or that. Anyway this 'king' met another 'king' on the mountaintop who recognized who he was, and blessed him and empowered him incredibly, one night, just talking." Sometimes the encounter can be extremely surprising, uplifting and powerful.

I remember having a participant in a workshop who was one of the most joyful and loving people I've ever met. Even when people teased her about her upbeat temperament, she wasn't deterred from her cheerfulness and positive manner. Her vibrant energy and love for people emanated from her like a radiant star, and her enthusiasm and accepting demeanor were a wonderful model for me, since I tend to be more serious and reserved. I learned how the sharing of joy and enthusiasm is a gift, and it moves me along my own path.

We may also find our teachers among our spiritual friends. When I asked Jan Hoffman, a Quaker, about spiritual teachers, she said, "I don't have just one. I have a whole network. I'll feel led at different times to call different ones, and I don't know why I call one over another. Other times one of them will call with a message they have been led to share with me in particular. Or I might get a postcard simply saying, 'When I took you into prayer this week, I felt a dimming of the light from your direction, so I will be holding you more firmly in God's Light.' From these experiences, I know I can trust that wider network to work." Bishop Murray Finck, in addition to having a spiritual director, has a very good spiritual friend: "We make sure that we spend some time together once a month to talk about these things. We don't give each other direction; we just have connection." I am grateful for having spiritual friends who support me in my practice. They remind me that at the heart of every spiritual practice is love and compassion, and have taught me what it means to love, and to be loved.

So pay attention: spiritual teachers can show up unexpectedly, with life-changing messages, and sometimes are gone almost as quickly as they appear. They also can be spiritual friends who share our journey and identify with our quest.

There are also "formal" spiritual teachers from whom most of us can benefit. These are spiritual guides, teachers or directors who work closely with us on a regular basis; who have experienced and understood what it means to pursue a spiritual path; who are willing and able to guide us on our journey; and who are there to support us and teach us when we get stuck or lose our way.

Attributes of a Spiritual Teacher

Since we're focusing on the formal student-teacher relationship, we should start with a general description of the spiritual guide or teacher. I like Pastor Preston Price's definition, and I think it generally describes the spiritual teachers whom I've met: "A spiritual teacher is someone eager to talk with you about your spiritual journey and to help you in numerous ways to develop a spiritual path."

Many of the people I interviewed for this book were either spiritual teachers or directors, or had their own spiritual teacher, or both. They spoke in depth about the attributes of a spiritual teacher, and although no one teacher may have all of these qualities, any teacher you engage should have many of them.

In describing the spiritual teacher, I use the terms spiritual guide, spiritual teacher and spiritual director interchangeably. Their attributes are divided somewhat arbitrarily into three areas: (1) role description, (2) internal qualities, and (3) interactive practices; I say the divisions are arbitrary, since some attributes in one category could fit into one of the other categories. By using these categories, however, I hope to focus on the many roles that a spiritual director must play, the personal characteristics and perspectives they must be able to draw on in order to develop a meaningful, productive and safe relationship with a student, and the versatility in behaviors they must demonstrate in order to be effective in helping the student along the spiritual path.

Role Description

The roles of the spiritual guide are complex and multifaceted. The guide needs to be a mentor, friend, teacher, role model, and a container for the spiritual life of the student.

Mentor

Mentoring was described in this way by Pastor Craig Lockwood: "My role is to understand people's gifting, their personal uniqueness, and to help them get where they need to go. And if they're in the wrong place, I help reflect reality to them in terms of 'maybe you're not really made for this, you could be made for that.' So I'm helping them as a mentor on a couple of levels: one is in their relationship with God, their personal transformation, and the second is in their role in the body of Christ. I'm helping them get into the right place, so they can be as fulfilled as they can be, and they can do what they're created to do. That's my role as a mentor."

Mentoring means filling the role of a guide, reflecting a person's gifts and aspirations, mirroring their hopes and desires for pursuing a spiritual life. It means letting go of the need to control other people, but rather reveal to them, or help them discover, more of who they are and what they have to offer to others.

Friend

Having a teacher who also is a friend on the journey is enormously comforting and reassuring. I see Jikyo Sensei as my spiritual friend, because I know that she deeply and sincerely cares about my spiritual journey and growth; she shares some of her own stories of struggle and desire, stories that remind me that I am never alone on this spiritual path. She is intimately human, as a woman who is not only a Zen priest and sensei, but a mother, wife, psychotherapist, dancer and artist, and she fully embraces whatever she is doing in that moment. She does not put herself above others, but often reflects on how she learns from all her students. She shares her aspirations, and she is intensely interested in helping her students realize their own. As she guides me on my spiritual journey, her devotion to the Zen Buddhist path and engagement with, and fondness for me as well as her other students is always apparent. When I experience her sincerity, warmth and sense of humor, as well as her wisdom and compassion, I am moved and touched at her investment in, and commitment to, our relationship. Paraphrasing the words of Linda Klassen, Protestant practitioner and counselor, and Father John McAndrew, Roman Catholic priest, *my teacher is truly a companion on my journey.*

Teacher

Probing, asking questions, sharing stories—these are often the ways my spiritual guide teaches me on the spiritual journey. When I am feeling desolate, bereft and sorry for myself, Jikyo Sensei often helps me shift my perspective. She will say, "What is it you're experiencing?" And I will answer, "Sadness." And she will say, "Think of all the people in the world who, at this moment, are feeling sad." And suddenly I am no longer alone but connected to and comforted by all those in the universe experiencing sadness. Or one time when I was complaining about another person's behavior, sensei asked me, "What does judging want?" And I answered, "I'm wanting that person to make better decisions!" And she will ask, "And what are the chances that will happen?" And I had to acknowledge, "Very little chance." My very acknowledgment released some of the desire and energy I had around that situation, and reminded me how often I try to control or modify the behaviors of others, when I am powerless to do that.

Swami Atmavidyananda describes the guru (Hindu word for "teacher")in this way: "A guru can help you adjust to a problem in practice. Problems arise, and if you're just doing it on your own, you don't know if you should just wait it out or if you need to make an adjustment. It's like trying to learn a musical instrument; you really need somebody to make sure you're not forgetting some aspect of practicing. You may need to make a simple adjustment in fingering the instrument or in your attitude or some other aspect that will help you play better. Similarly in spiritual life you can use help in getting through the problems that arise."

A good teacher doesn't take only a didactic approach to spiritual guidance. Rabbi Steve Robbins says of spiritual teachers, "The word rabbi or rav simply means a master or a teacher, no more holy, no less holy or meaningful than you are. He or she is only a teacher and a guide. Teachers should not try to put you into their mold, but have you find yours. The teacher must understand that it is not about the teacher or what the teacher knows; it is about the student and what he or she knows. It is not what you teach them, but as you guide and instruct them, you are revealing what is *already* planted within them, not what you're planting in them."

Role Model

Some people make the mistake of looking for a spiritual guide who is perfect, which will never happen. The spiritual guide instead serves as a role model for pursuing the spiritual journey, representing all that is both human and divine, strong and weak, serene and agitated, faithful and skeptical, wise and naïve, compassionate and intolerant. The most skilled spiritual guides continually aspire to deepen their spiritual lives, live lives of integrity and courage, and are astutely aware of their limitations—and are not afraid to acknowledge them. People I spoke to for this book readily volunteered their struggles, or weaknesses, or doubts that are part of the spiritual journey. And they also spoke to their ceaseless efforts to emulate the Divine, or work with their limitations, or grow in their intimate relationships with God or the universal Spirit.

My Zen teacher, by allowing me to see all of who she is (which doesn't mean everything about her, but rather a full spectrum of her essentialness) continually models for me the beauty of the path: the paradox of accepting that on one level, I am whole and complete as I am, and on another level, I aspire to deepen my understanding of my complex being, and in so doing, *comprehend* who I truly am and deepen and bring integrity to my spiritual life.

A Container

Sometimes the mystery of the spiritual life and the confusion about where we are going is more than we are able to comprehend and handle on our own. It's as if, at times, the life of spirit is more than one person can grasp and embrace, and thus the teacher serves as a container, a companion who can help us hold ourselves up and help us maintain a framework for living the spiritual life. Nicolee Jikyo McMahon Sensei says, "I can look at myself, at the beginning, doing spiritual practices by myself and not working with a teacher; the difference between those times and when I began working with a teacher was so profound that I can't find a way to describe it. It's like living in the desert versus having access to the world; that was the difference for me when I began to study with a teacher who'd walked the path before me and was helping me open my understanding."

The spiritual journey is immensely rewarding at times, but it is not easy. At times I have felt close to God, and at other times I have felt alone and isolated. Sometimes I overflow with the richness of Spirit, and at other times life seems mundane and ordinary. Then there are those times when life rolls along at a manageable clip, things seem to be going well, and suddenly everything seems to fall apart. All of this is my life, and at times I feel like I am reeling under the staggering weight of my perceptions, as if I were carrying a towering armload of packages that are far too heavy, a tower that is so tall that it blocks my vision of the path. Those are the times when my spiritual guide can help.

Although the concept of the container is difficult to describe, it is profoundly valuable. In one respect, the teacher creates for us a permeable, invisible, spiritual dwelling that allows us to interact with the world, and also somehow creates a place of safety and reassurance. The Rev. Lois McAfee explains, "The spiritual director's job is more like a receptacle holding this person safely and caringly in time and place, while he or she and God commune." The spiritual guide is at any given time a witness, a place of refuge, solace, wisdom and caring, a spiritual companion and a container for our engagement with God.

Internal Qualities

In addition to taking on several roles, spiritual guides share certain internal characteristics that help them develop rapport and trusting relationships with students. Some of the attributes that cannot be seen easily, but are internal and invaluable to the spiritual teacher include the ability to be present, humility, and non-attachment.

Ability to Be Present

Spiritual guides have as many, if not more demands on their lives than their students. They have occupations, families, friends, community commitments, just like we do. Lots of activities and people demand their time; yet when meeting with a student, an effective spiritual guide is able to let go of distractions and preoccupations, in order to be fully present.

Being present doesn't mean forgetting everything else going on in your life. It means including everything in your life in every moment, yet when you are teaching, you are *just teaching,* and when you are being a wife, you are *just being a wife,* and when you are being a friend, you are *simply being a friend.* In the moment when you engage with an activity or a person, you are emotionally, intellectually, and spiritually present. Nothing else matters except this moment of exchange; everything else fades in importance compared to what is occurring between you and whatever or whomever is in front of you.

When I am in interview with Jikyo Sensei, I feel as if, in those moments, our dialogue is of uppermost importance, that she is fully attentive to helping me explore my spiritual practice, that whatever other demands are tugging on her consciousness have been set aside for our intimate dialogue. She is one of the busiest persons I know, but she seems to embrace her life fully, no matter what she is doing. And when I am sitting before her, those moments have both of us fully engaged, and our energies are focused on my latest struggle, or insight, or frustration, or question.

Being present means that a spiritual teacher is fully absorbed in whatever the focus of my practice is, *in that moment.* Whether I'm struggling with the same issue for the fifteenth time, or wondering how I can keep from falling asleep on my zafu (sitting pillow), my teacher treats the issue with respect and concern. When I am regretting the past or worrying about the future, my spiritual teacher brings me back to the present, to the here and now; she reminds me that I cannot change the past, but can learn from it; that I cannot control the future, but can plan for it.

It takes discipline and empathy for a teacher to be fully present, and I'm sure there are times when all of them feel as if they've heard the same complaint one time too many, or they are tired, impatient or preoccupied. But for the most part, a skilled spiritual guide will be able to put all of that aside and make each moment count.

Humility

"I find that being a spiritual director is powerful, moving and humbling. It's not scary, but I find I have to be very dependent on God. I have to get out of the way and be an instrument of God's love." The Rev. Charlotte Cleghorn, Episcopal priest shared these thoughts about humility and the spiritual guide. Rabbi Steve Robbins says, "A teacher must be kind and thoughtful and humble, and must be grateful to the students who come to him or her for being permitted to teach. The teacher must always be aware that what he or she is doing contains in it great arrogance; it is chutzpah at its utmost to assume that you can teach anybody, or that you have the right or the skill to do it."

Swami Sarvadevananda gives a description of a Vedanta guru: "Who is a guru? One who knows the scriptures, who is living a pure life, who is not motivated by name, money or position. He is a realized soul, or at least a person who has been practicing for 60 or 70 years, and who acts out of love for the disciple."

Unfortunately, there are spiritual teachers who go beyond recognizing the divine in themselves and in others; they begin to believe that *they are* the divine. When spiritual teachers make decisions that serve themselves and not their students, or try to violate personal boundaries, or make unethical decisions, they have lost the gift of humility. They have forgotten that ultimately they are teachers because they choose to serve, not be served. Instead, they have chosen to elevate themselves at the expense of others; they have become delusional about their roles and their abilities, the same as any spiritual practitioner can.

In contrast, I remember hearing Jikyo Sensei talk about Maezumi Roshi, her teacher, and what was so extraordinary about him was how ordinary he was; he was a very gifted teacher, and as human and authentic as his students. I also greatly admire Jikyo Sensei, and am often moved by her ability to connect with a wisdom that I still see as far beyond me, while she also tells us about her struggles with the same things the rest of us face—finding enough time to do everything, taking care of herself, finding time to rest. Also, rather than isolating themselves or assuming they have all the answers, both Jikyo Sensei and her senior student and Zen priest, John Jiyu Gage welcome creative ideas; to them, feedback is a source of enthusiasm, curiosity and exploration, and new approaches from students feed the growth and maturation of our innovative community.

Spiritual guides who understand humility understand that they are as human and vulnerable as the next person. They realize that because it is easy to go astray, they must make themselves available to hearing if they have abandoned humility for conceit, either by welcoming the guidance of their own teachers or the input of their communities. Spiritual teachers who are willing to not only guide others, but are receptive to guidance from others when they get off track, can find their way back to the vision of the spiritual teacher, and may be better teachers for having strayed off the path and having learned and appreciated the lessons that have been offered.

Non-Attachment

An effective spiritual guide knows how to maintain the tension and balance of non-attachment and involvement. The term "non-attachment" has gotten a bad rap. Many people think the term means "not caring" or "not being involved." "Non-attachment" is also different from "detachment"; detachment means *to separate* or *disengage*; non-attachment means finding the balance of being empathic, concerned about and invested in helping another, but not becoming emotionally entangled in issues in a way that prevents one from objectively and appropriately helping. When a teacher becomes overly invested in and emotional about a student's situation, he or she cannot help from a place of genuine caring, perspective and wisdom.

A spiritual guide understands what you are going through, not because he is experiencing the same emotions you are experiencing in a given moment, but because *he has walked the same path that you are walking.* Your particular concerns or questions may not be identical to those he has struggled with, but they are companions to the spiritual questions that all of us face. While an insightful spiritual guide will empathize and grasp where you are on your journey, he needs to be capable of comprehending that although he can identify with your experience, he is not witnessing his own experience re-manifesting in that moment.

When we receive guidance from our spiritual teachers, they need to be able to create some distance from their own experiences when they are similar to ours, and not be misguided by the intensity of the feelings that might be stirred up from their own journeys; otherwise they can become confused about who is struggling and suffering, and mistake our pain for their own. They need to be able to transform their passion and emotions into compassion and wisdom; their assistance must come from a source of understanding and clarity, not from the distortion and personalization of our experiences into their own. Their abilities to relate to our experiences must not be overshadowed by their own agendas; that relatedness must be used as a tool to access spiritual truth and personal experience to help us comprehend and develop in our own unique spiritual journeys.

Interactive Practices

In addition to the roles they play and their internal attributes, the most effective spiritual guides demonstrate certain key qualities. They are versatile, knowing how to modify their interactions with students based on the student's temperament and the situation; they are good listeners, hearing what is being said and what has not been said; and they know how to reveal the divine in students, so that students can see the divine within themselves.

Versatility

The Rev. John Jiyu Gage describes the versatility of the teacher this way: "If spiritual guides or teachers are really worth their salt, they need to be willing to be whatever is required at a given point in time, and know what the student is needing. You may be a loving parent, a harsh taskmaster or just a good friend. It totally depends on where the student is and his or her level of practice. It's a constant going-back-and-forth and being able to know what to say or do, or how to apply the teaching at a particular point in time, because the student's needs are always shifting and changing."

I remember one time I was visiting Rabbi Jonathan Omer-Man about some questions I had regarding the Jewish aspects of my spiritual practice. Near the end of our discussion, I explained that I was going on a one-week Zen intensive retreat. (He already knew that I had a daily spiritual practice, and that I was struggling with how to honor my Jewish roots and my Zen beliefs.) I asked him if there was anything else I could do at the intensive retreat that would include my Jewish practice, beyond the morning and evening prayers I was doing. He looked at me for a moment and said, "I think you have enough to do." He hesitated, then continued, "You see, this is how I work: when I see students who are not making the effort, I load them up with work; for those who are working hard, I leave them be. You have enough to do." I felt the tears in my eyes at his response; I was trying so hard to develop a spiritual life of integrity, and he not only made me feel enormously relieved that there was no need to take on another task, but he also honored the sincerity and commitment of my spiritual efforts. Contrast his kindness to his description of himself as a teacher: "I belong to the rather tough, abrasive school of being a teacher, and any idea that the teacher is just honey and smiles is not the teacher I've ever had, or any teacher I could ever emulate. Ultimately a teacher provides what needs to be beckoned, confronted, molded or liberated." I've no doubt that Rabbi Omer-Man can be tough, but he also knows when the situation calls for kindness, and he has the ability to provide that as well.

Regardless of the nature or personality of the teacher, he or she must be versatile enough to know what the student needs, and what will best help the student when he or she stumbles or is lost on the path. The ability to shift perspective, attitude and approach at a moment's notice is what makes the teacher most powerful and makes the teachings so profound.

Listening

For many of us, listening is an incredibly difficult task. To truly listen requires an earlier attribute described: being present. But listening requires much more than that. It requires us to put away our internal voice, the voice that continually critiques, evaluates and judges what people are saying, and leaves us incapable of truly hearing what is being said.

Genuine listening by a spiritual teacher requires him or her to silence the judging voice, empathize, and hear more than what is being said; they need at times to be able to discern the underlying message that even we might not be aware of. As the Rev. Charlotte Cleghorn, Episcopal priest says, "I try to listen to all the things being said *and not being said* to help a person on his or her journey." When spiritual guides listen, they must also communicate that they are engaged, both physically and verbally. Their body language should invite your sharing: open body posture, eye contact, and comments that let you know that they are fully attentive. By listening, they are able to engage you in a way that helps you ponder your own questions and even perceive your own answers.

When we are genuinely listened to, we also experience with the teacher a connectedness of mind and spirit, know that the teacher in front of us cares and is invested in helping us appreciate and grow in our spiritual development. Their ability to listen validates that we have something worthwhile to say, that our suffering has meaning, and that our experience is not separate from, but rather connects us to, others in the universe.

Seeing the Divine

Helping us to see the Divine in each person, and all around us, is also part of the task of the spiritual director. So often we may see ourselves as isolated or separate from God, whether it is experiencing the absence of God within ourselves or the absence of God around us. The Rev. Margie Clark comments, "My first role is to see the Divine in people, because I sincerely believe that's one way we open doors. When I see the Divine in others, it helps them to see the Divine in themselves." In these times, people can be very demanding of themselves, and very self-critical. They don't realize that being flawed is partly what it means to be human; and it is our very humanness that allows us to open to the Divine aspects of ourselves, our abilities to be compassionate, to uplift, to serve.

We also may forget that God is more than what we could ever imagine, beyond description, beyond attributes, beyond limits. The Rev. Murray Finck states, "The qualities of a spiritual director include helping another to see where God is in all things." God is not only never separate from ourselves; God is never separate from anything, and exists everywhere, in every moment, beyond time, transcending description, surpassing understanding, and yet intimate and available right here, right now. When we not only understand and believe that, but genuinely experience the pervading presence of God, we open our lives to limitless spiritual potential and peace.

The Process of Spiritual Guidance

There are a number of strategies spiritual guides use to help sojourn-ers along the way. A primary approach is discernment, which includes helping us explore our circumstances, providing us with options, and supplying us with tools to help us find direction. Discernment is the ability to discover that which connects us with the divine and com-prehending that which separates us.

Exploring our Circumstances

The spiritual guide helps you reflect on and learn from your spiritual life. One way to pursue this exploration is by the spiritual teacher's trying to clarify the student's experience. The Rev. Charlotte Cleghorn explains: "Spiritual direction is not about fixing anything. It's about honoring the movement of God in another person's life, and reflecting that back, and sometimes helping to clarify something that might be very confusing. I've had people say, 'nothing much is happening this week,' and I'll say, 'tell me a little bit,' and then they'll tell me about some little thing that happened that ends up being massive and pro-found."

Spiritual directors help you deepen your practice, when you're stuck in skating the surface of your experience. Sometimes we are blinded to our own reality, or frightened to go beyond the obvious, or uncomfortable witnessing what is really reinforcing our resistance to following the path. Linda Klassen says, "We need outside, objective help in this whole area to understand what's really going on. A spiritual director helps me to discern some current experience that I may be blinded to, and may be able to determine what it might be about, because I'm just too close to it to discern that."

Pursuing a spiritual path is not inherently confusing or overwhelming, but because our lives are complex, we overcomplicate spirituality and erect a multitude of self-generated barriers to practice. Spiritual teachers use many talents and resources to work through those barriers; sometimes they help us tap away at them persistently and continually; at other times, a word or even a moment of silence in guidance extinguishes the roadblocks we have worked so hard to erect. Either way, this exploration of our spiritual practices moves us along the path to discovering ourselves, and God.

Providing us with Options

We often have the answers to our spiritual questions, but we are so bound up in our self-imposed limitations, that we think our answers and opportunities are finite, or don't even exist. A spiritual guide can help us see beyond our narrow framework and expand the possibilities of options for action or learning. The Rev. Margie Clark says, "I'm inclined to let people work things out when they have issues; I don't give a lot of suggestions, and I train other spiritual counselors that we never give advice, but we do give options. Most of us get locked into one way of being or thinking, and one of the greatest gifts that we can give people is to say, 'Have you thought of this, or if you tried this, what would happen?' This approach gets people 'unlocked' and it's important to get people to think outside their boxes."

Spiritual teachers cannot make things right for us. Anne Seisen Saunders, Sensei says, "The teacher's function is not to do the work for a student, or to give him or her enlightenment. The teacher is like a coach and each person does it for himself or herself, and each person finds his or her own path. Teachers can't tell anybody exactly how to do it, but we can see when people are slipping, and say, 'Okay, you're

holding on here, you're holding on there,' and that's our function."
Karen Goran, spiritual director has a similar view: "Sometimes the
role of the spiritual director is to help people see what their blocks
are, or explore their feelings around the blocks. Eventually you might
make suggestions about the way people can let go of the blocks. But I
don't think you can just dive in to fix them up."

Your spiritual development is up to you, and spiritual guides can
help you along the way. They are not available to "fix you" or solve
your problems. Although they counsel, they are not acting as thera-
pists; they're job is not to make you psychologically whole, although
sometimes (not always) that is an outcome of practice. You need to
remember that in the end, you are responsible for how far you travel
on your own spiritual path, and how deep and rich your practice
becomes.

Supplying us with Tools

Jikyo Sensei has provided me with many tools to develop my spiritual
practice, to help me witness my own true nature and oneness with
the universe. In Zen practice, koan training and mindfulness training
are just two of the tools that I have used to develop a personal spiritual practice.

Spiritual teachers can provide you with development tools, based
on your temperament and development. The Rev. Preston Price shares
his approach to providing tools in spiritual direction: "Some people
want a recipe; others almost want a guarantee or a quick fix, but I
need to know them better. They need to know themselves, too, and
find out what things do and don't work for them. So I listen to the
kinds of persons they are, what's been working for them, what their
backgrounds are, and build on that. That's a creative process, and it's
exciting to do. I worked with one person where all we did was pray
together, and I've had others where we've talked, experimented and
I've given them assignments, and they've come back in two weeks and
told me how that's working." It takes time to determine the right tools,
and a spiritual teacher will want to spend the time to develop the relationship and learn what will work best for you.

Selecting a Spiritual Guide

Up to this point, we've described the attributes of a teacher, but it's important also to suggest precautions to take in selecting a spiritual guide. My concern, particularly with Westerners, is that they either refuse to develop an honest and committed relationship with a teacher, or (much worse), they give themselves up entirely to a person of poor or little repute, and risk serious emotional, spiritual and psychological damage. "You should choose a teacher with the same amount of caution with which you buy a used car: get some pedigree; ask them who their teachers were. There are teachers who have no teachers, but if you meet someone who has no pedigree, no lineage, be doubly cautious—buyer beware. Don't hand them your credit cards and check book in the first 15 minutes." Rabbi Omer-Man shared these thoughts with me, and I very much agree with him.

So how can you screen and select a teacher who is trustworthy, qualified and a match for you on the spiritual path? I asked this question of a number of teachers, and one of the most comprehensive responses came from Anne Seisen Saunders, Sensei of Sweetwater Zen Center. I'd like to quote her responses in italics, and then add my own thoughts.

1. *If the teacher says he will do the work for you, or gives you the impression that the only way to attain enlightenment is hanging around with him—that's delusional. The teacher should be reinforcing that* you *are the primary source for your spiritual development.* There are many teachers who are available to guide you in your spiritual practice, and an alarm should go off in your head if any teacher says she has exclusive access to the way.

2. *If the teacher says this is the only way, that's a red flag.* This kind of statement may be a warning that the teacher represents not a religion, but a cult. His or her vision, rather than being one of universal wisdom and love, may represent a parochial and exclusive view of spirituality. Most religions have certain universal truths that cross all religions of integrity.

3. *If the teacher says she has reached a place where she no longer needs to practice anymore, that's a warning sign, because practice is for life.* The Buddha or Jesus may have been enlightened beings, but I'd assume that any teachers you meet haven't gotten there yet. They may have learned to handle many of their challenges more productively if their practice is mature, but a relationship with God, or connection with the universe and an evolving spiritual practice is a lifetime commitment.

4. *If a teacher portrays himself as completely pure and above human frailty, that would be a warning for me!* Only that which is beyond the human, that is Spirit, is above human frailty.

5. *How do you feel with this teacher? Do you feel a connection? Do you feel comfortable, safe to some degree?* Sometimes our intuition tells us that we are not a match with a teacher. There are lots of good teachers, and you shouldn't try to work with someone who, even over time, causes you to feel uncomfortable or unsafe.

6. *Get over the search for the perfect teacher! It's the same as a marriage. We don't find our partner until we get over the search for the perfect one! Once you've found that person, make a commitment.* If you are looking for the teacher who is greater than human, who has no flaws, no troubles, no struggles, you will eternally be disappointed. What's important is to make sure that the flaws are not fatal: that their troubles do not interfere with their ability to work with you, and that their struggles don't make them spiritually unavailable to be present for you.

7. *If a teacher wants to take credit for your spiritual development, that's a problem: you're the one who has done the work.* This concern goes to the teacher inflating her role in your spiritual development, as well as not reinforcing that you are the one who can take credit for doing the work and making the effort.

8. *Be cautious about what a teacher requests. If a teacher asks for sex, or too much of your time, or too much money, he or she is*

likely a false teacher. I know that I am continually evaluating the amount of time I spend on my spiritual practice, and the time it takes me away from my work and my husband. There are times when I would love to go to a sesshin, but it conflicts with an important family obligation. At those times, the family wins; there will always be other retreats.

9. *There are times when the teacher will ask you to do something that makes you uncomfortable, which usually involves letting go of your delusional self. You need to test your level of trust with this person, and whether you believe the person is speaking with your best interests in mind.* Earlier in this book I related the story of my teacher asking me to continue working on a koan when I did not want to, but I continued anyway. Or sometimes at sesshin I've been asked to be timekeeper of the meditation periods or sensei's attendant, which can distract me at times from focusing on my meditation practice. I can either resist these requests, or I can accept them and look into the nature of my resistance—why am I unwilling to see these roles as part of my practice? Am I not striving everyday to maintain my spiritual life in the midst of other demands and responsibilities? Isn't this a great opportunity to practice blending spiritual practice with the expectations of my every day life?

10. *If you really feel like you don't want to do something right now, then wait and develop the trust. When you say instantly that you will do whatever your teacher says, that's dangerous. There's time to build trust with a teacher.* It's important not to elevate your teacher to a degree where you abandon your ability to make wise decisions. Both times I have had a spiritual teacher, I have taken my time to build trust. And if I was uncomfortable with expectations or some aspect of the relationship, we talked about it; these moments can be very rewarding and trust-building, when you are willing to talk about the nature of your relationship.

Some additional thoughts regarding the selection of a spiritual teacher: ask other students what they see as the attributes and drawbacks of working with a particular teacher . . . ask the teacher her perspective on the student-teacher relationship, what she expects, how she works with students, what happens when you disagree, and any other concerns that you have . . . find out what kind of commitment he expects in terms of time, resources and participation in spiritual activities of the community. . . the key is to make sure as you begin to work with the teacher that the perceptions, assumptions and conclusions you have drawn about your practice and teacher are legitimate, so that you don't damage a relationship due to misunderstandings or fear.

Rabbi Steve Robbins shared a wonderful story about the teacher-student relationship:

> My ancestor, Isaac Luria, had a great student come to him and wanted to study with him, and he avoided seeing him, wouldn't see him, for weeks. And finally the student trapped him and asked, "Why won't you see me?" And Luria said, "If I see you, it will be my impulse to teach you, because you are such a brilliant student, but I know that what I have to teach you is not what you need to know in this world. Your path lies someplace else, and I'm not meant to be your teacher. Go find your teacher." And the student said, "But master, everybody is learning from you." And Luria said, "No, not everybody learns from me. Those who are meant to learn from me will find me. And there are those who find me who are not meant to learn from me. Go find your teacher." The man left, and became a great Talmudist. He was not meant to be a Kabbalist in this world; he was meant to do something else. So not everybody who comes to me should learn from me. Part of my responsibility is to suggest to people, "Maybe this isn't where you ought to be." And it's the responsibility of the student to say, "I'm not satisfied with what I'm learning," and for the teacher to then say, "Maybe I'm just not meant to be your teacher."

In the teacher-student relationship, you have a responsibility for choosing your teacher, but your teacher also chooses you. As Seisen, Sensei explained, "I think a marriage is a nice analogy. We go through courtship, and we ask questions and we watch, and then we say, 'Okay,

I'm going with this.' Then we commit and we really work on the relationship. Then to dissolve the relationship is a really big deal, and we think about it pretty hard before we do it."

The role of the spiritual director, his or her attributes and skills can be a powerful catalyst to the development of your spiritual life. You can choose to abandon your religion because of your history; or insist on pursuing a spiritual life on your own; or simply spend the rest of your life wondering what you are missing. Or you can find a spiritual guide, someone who is there to nurture and support you, a companion who has walked the same path, a coach and facilitator, a mentor and teacher, who is there to help you test the ocean of the spiritual voyage and when you're ready, help you jump into the vast and mysterious waters with an open heart. The spiritual guide is available to not only develop a close relationship with you; he is there to help you learn to be intimate with yourself, intimate with God, intimate with your life.

CHAPTER SEVEN

What is the Role of Being of Service?

The main problem of service is to be the way without being "in the way." And if there are any tools, techniques and skills to be learned they are primarily to plow the field, to cut the weeds and to clip the branches, that is, to take away the obstacles for real growth and development.
~ HENRI NOUWEN, *Reaching Out*

K ue and I drove to Escondido today. She is recovering from a fall, and had to visit several doctors. I was so glad to be with her and to have a chance to help. I read while I waited for her, thinking periodically of how she has talked about the effect of her injury on her life view. Kue has shared what being injured has taught her, how it has made her slow down, pay attention and appreciate the value of compassion for others. How wonderful, that she can move beyond the pain and inconvenience of her accident, and reflect on and appreciate lessons learned. I have also reflected on what it means to me to be able to help her, how being with her touches my life, and how I feel the presence of Spirit in our time together. We enjoyed a lunch of pizza and salad between appointments, sharing our life stories; my life seems so ordinary compared to her own experiences. I admire her resilience and determina-

tion, in spite of her many physical setbacks. I may be the one pro-viding the transportation and support today, but there is no doubt that in our conversations, laughter and commiseration, we are truly serving each other.

———————————————————●———————————————————

Being of service is a deepening process in the evolution and matu-ration of the spiritual path. We begin as "baby bodhisattvas"; in Bud-dhism, bodhisattvas are compassionate beings who postpone final enlightenment for the sake of helping others. When we see ourselves as bodhisattvas, we realize that at different stages along the spiritual path we give up and gain something in order to serve others; what we give up, and what we gain both change as our spiritual practices de-velop and mature.

In talking about the role of service in deepening our spiritual lives, we will look at providing service through the window of the six *paramitas*, attitudes and behaviors practiced by the bodhisattva on the path to realization. We will observe how service practice manifests in its infancy, and that as our service practices deepen, so does our spiri-tual life; correspondingly, as our spiritual practices deepen, the na-ture of being of service also ripens. We'll also study how one can decide how to be of service, how to watch for pitfalls in serving others, and how being of service to others transforms Spirit in our lives.

Looking Through the Window of Service

Imagine looking out a garden window and noticing two new sprigs of ivy climbing up a tall wooden trellis; the sprigs appear to be fol-lowing their own spiraling patterns, independently stretching for the sunshine and soaking up the spring rain. But one day, many months later, you look out the window again and suddenly realize that they are no longer sprigs, but have become vines: intertwined, hearty and inseparable. And because of the green tapestry they have created with their offspring of tendrils and leaves, you no longer see them as inde-pendent, at all. Their lives as separate sprigs have transformed into an integrated, interdependent existence.

When talking about being of service and spiritual practice, particularly if we are novices on the spiritual path, it is easy to describe them as separate but related paths. Part of the reason may be that in the early stages of our efforts to serve, we are devoting our time to others, and we are also losing that time for other activities. No matter how helpful we want to be, no matter how moved we are to serve others, being of service can also be inconvenient, frustrating, and difficult, particularly when we are new to the spiritual path. We may also volunteer to serve out of a sense of duty, or because it makes us feel good. *None of these attitudes and emotions is wrong or bad.* They are simply descriptive of the fragile and emerging effort of the novice to be of service.

As we move along the spiritual path, however, our experience of being of service begins to transform. We move through a conversion experience, conversion as it is translated to mean, "turn around"; we become aware of ourselves serving in a different light, not out of obligation, but because we are called to serve and relate to others in new and compassionate ways.

One way of looking at being of service is through the window of the six paramitas, the attitudes and behaviors of the bodhisattva who lives to relieve the suffering of others. The six paramitas are generosity, discipline, patience, effort, meditation and wisdom, universal values that appear in every major religion. These six attributes are present from the moment that we begin to practice lives of service, but our experience of them, and their manifestation in our attempts to relate and be helpful to others evolves and matures as we move along the spiritual path. Although I describe each paramita separately, they, like the ivy vines, are interrelated and inseparable; when we focus on the practice of one paramita, we influence all of them. In looking at each of the six paramitas and understanding how each one may be underused, misused or suitably manifested in our efforts to serve, we can begin to understand how finding a balance of intention and action is our charge in merging service with our spiritual lives, and that being of service is a process in deepening our relationship with God.

Generosity

I remember one Sunday afternoon when I was helping Kue with her computer; it was originally my old computer, which I had donated to the Zen Center and which the Center had loaned to her. Kue was trying to use e-mail, and setting up the program was giving her trouble. I worked with her for three or four hours that afternoon, and decided to head home when we learned that a download of software was going to take four hours. I assured her that everything would be fine, and that I would call her, but as soon as I walked out the door, I had misgivings. Part of me wanted to just go home, light the fire in the fireplace and have a quiet dinner; but there was a morsel of me that wanted to not only help Kue, but to be with her if she ran into trouble. As I drove towards home, the morsel in me grew, until it enveloped my heart; I got off at the next freeway exit and without a moment of regret, headed back to Kue's apartment. When her quiet voice answered my knock on her door, and I saw her beaming face when she let me in, I had all the confirmation that I needed that I was in the right place.

Generosity is probably the paramita I struggle with the most. I not only feel stingy at times about volunteering my time; I worry about raising people's expectations about how helpful I am willing to be, or whether someone may try to take advantage of me. It also raises questions for me about intimacy, about how close I want to be to other people in my life.

When we begin to work with generosity in terms of serving others, we have a unique opportunity to notice how we feel about being generous: is it important that others see us as generous? Does it feed our egos and desire to be seen as generous people? Is there a part of us that feels just a little superior to others because we are in service?

Are we being of service in areas that we don't enjoy? Do we not serve because we have many other commitments that we see as too important to give up? Or do we donate so much of our time that our families suffer and we burn out from the demands on our time? These are sometimes difficult questions to answer, because we may think they will reveal our weaker, selfish selves. But instead of seeing our answers in a judgmental light, we should examine our answers with generosity for ourselves, and ask what the answers can teach us. They lead us to other helpful questions: what amount of time in serving others would be generous for me, based on my life circumstances and how I have given to others in the past? What activities would not only help others but would also fill my soul space? It's helpful to remember that when we give to others, we also give to ourselves; the gratitude and appreciation of others is an offering that fills our hearts. And when we give to others and receive in return, all of it is a gift from and to God.

Generosity also applies to our *receiving from* others. I have a lovely, gifted and generous friend, who has told me she is uncomfortable when others thank her for her help. Generosity in accepting others' gratitude is also a gift to them, because it tells them that our hearts have connected in invisible and irresistible circuits of love. When we are willing to open to that love, we invite God to revel in our relationships, too.

When we are generous in serving others, we deepen our spirituality, too. Too often we may feel we are distant from God or we miss our connectedness to the universe. We often suffer from self-centeredness and constriction, an unwillingness to open our hearts. As our generosity matures, we gradually start to realize that our isolation is a manifestation of our own anxious minds; instead of judging ourselves, we can begin to forgive our human limitations. When we serve others in generous ways, we often begin to experience ourselves softening and our hearts melting, opening a pathway to the universal; we open ourselves up to intimacy with those we love and in our relationship with God. More and more we generously invite God to enter our lives and experience God as present—and we begin to understand that we are never alone.

Discipline

Discipline comes from the word "disciple," which means student. We have so much that we can learn from being of service, but we have to be receptive to the lessons that it offers. Unfortunately, as I discussed in the chapter on commitment, many people perceive the word "discipline" as unappealing and restrictive. The irony is that discipline as a part of being of service to others has an essential and liberating quality; it allows us to move beyond our perceptions of who we are, what we think we should be doing, and what we have to offer.

Discipline means making the effort to learn what serving others means to us, in both spiritual and practical terms. It means deciding what we'd like to do, what we are called to do, what we are willing to do, and following through; and even when we find the assignment difficult or unappealing, we can appreciate what it has to teach us. It means showing up even when we don't feel like it, honoring our promise to help.

I spent a couple of years volunteering to help patients and nurses in a local hospital. I loved chatting with patients and running errands for the nurses; those were the fun and most enjoyable parts of the job. Part of the job also included getting snacks from the kitchen for the nurses' station refrigerators where they kept food ready for patients. The job meant going to the kitchen, loading up everything from milk to ice cream to soft drinks, carting the food back to the area I worked in, pulling the outdated food out of the refrigerator, and putting the new food in. Most of the time I enjoyed doing this job, too, its hands-on simplicity. Yes, there were times when the work seemed mundane and boring, and there were days that I noted my negative reactions with amusement. Instead of dwelling on my feelings, positive or negative, I simply noted my perceptions and I engaged in the task as a practice of mindfulness, really paying attention to every part of the process. I tried to remember how my simple tasks provided moments of relief for harried nurses, sustenance for frightened patients, and ultimately (indirectly) contributed to the healing of others.

Every time we commit to an act of service, we have the opportunity to immerse ourselves in every aspect of the task, especially those parts that we wouldn't ordinarily like. We have a chance to experience the task fully, to notice our reactions to it—boredom, pleasure, curiosity, frustration—and to do it to the best of our abilities. Discipline is the aspect of practice that holds us to our promise to be available and present, even when we don't feel fully engaged. And when, over time, we free ourselves from the illusion that our negative and judgmental thoughts *define* our actions of service, and realize that our perceptions are fleeting and ephemeral, we come to fully appreciate our reactions to our tasks and our commitment to do them, regardless of our perceptions. We are also humbled that others have allowed us the chance to offer our personal gifts.

Discipline in serving others parallels and supports a deepening spirituality, too. When we learn the discipline of paying attention and being present, those lessons teach us how to make the time for, and how to focus on Spirit. When we are most crazed and unable to be present, our discipline helps us to lay the past to rest and forego the future for just this moment, and we come face-to-face with our own lives, right now. Nicolee Miller McMahon, Sensei likes to remind me of the famous koan, "Not knowing is the most intimate." When we remain open to our unfolding lives, no matter what may occur, we feel connected to life in the most profound and intimate way.

Patience

Although my work frequently puts me in the center of groups of people, I basically work alone. I may seek the input of my husband, colleagues or friends regarding decisions for my business, but those decisions are solely mine. In the past, serving on boards of directors and committees has not been my favorite way to be of service, because it involves listening, sharing, negotiating, and relying on others. And lots of patience. There are frankly plenty of times, particularly if I am tired or frustrated, that I am not the least bit interested in knowing what somebody else wants to do; I just want to get through the meeting as quickly and as efficiently as possible. There is also the part of me that thinks I have the best answer to a situation, so why waste my time listening to what others have to say! And these are precisely the reasons why serving on committees and boards are, for me, a wonderful service practice in patience.

Committee meetings have brought up all my issues around wanting to be in control and having difficulty being empathic. When I find myself becoming impatient at a board meeting, I realize that my reaction is a wonderful opportunity for practice—what is this impatience?

Am I so certain that others don't need to be heard? Am I missing important points in the discussion because my mind is busy grumbling over the digressions and passions of the participants? What is it that I'm wanting? As I answer these questions, I remind myself, first, to breathe . . . just breathe. My focus on breathing allows me to slow down, let go of time concerns and start to open to what I am experiencing, what is being expressed and what is underneath others' words—a fear, a disappointment, a dream. Suddenly I realize the tension of impatience has begun to dissolve, and I am once again engaged. Instead of contracting both physically and mentally, I feel myself opening, like a clenched fist unfolding to an open palm, like a blooming rose breathing into the early morning light. Over time, I have found that I spend less time needing to study the nature of impatience, and instead, simply find my center and breathe into it. Expansiveness grows and awareness emerges, and listening and empathy are allowed to be born.

When we open to patience, we help ourselves to be attentive and receptive. As we serve others, we often cannot control unfolding events, and we may compromise our opportunity to serve when we succumb to negative perceptions or harmful behavior. Instead, we can transform impatience into curiosity and reflection: what is happening here? What do these circumstances and my reactions to them tell me about life? About myself? How can I remain present and compassionate with those I serve so that we can be together constructively? Or if I need to speak up, how can I use patience to make a point, to be loving, to move forward, to learn?

In terms of our spiritual development, the more we work with patience, and the more we are willing to integrate our learning into our spirit, the less we have to ask ourselves these questions. Gradually, imperceptibly, we notice ourselves relaxing, opening, listening and responding, without anxiety or impatience. We are simply engaged, purveyors of patience, as we serve others. And when we learn to be patient with others, we learn how to be patient with ourselves, and we open ourselves to the mysteries of the Infinite.

Effort

How much time should you spend volunteering? And what should you do? In regard to service, "right effort," meaning the right time, activity, and amount, is important. To be of service, you need to be available, not just physically, but mentally, spiritually and emotionally, too. That means finding a balance among the types of service and the amount of time you are giving to them.

I find that committing to a variety of service projects helps me create the balance I need in my life. Being on a Board of Directors of the Zen Center allows me the opportunity to develop deeper relationships with some of the people in the community. It also allows me to have a sense of continuity and growth, both in my efforts to help our community mature, and in my own personal development. As board membership changes, I learn how to experience the loss of old members and nurture intimacy with new ones. As a group, we are challenged to be creative and to expand our perceptions of what it means to be a spiritual community.

I also like the opportunity to help out as needed, whether I am helping a member of the community or serving on a temporary committee. I get a lot of satisfaction out of starting and finishing things, out of breaking my regular daily patterns, out of rising to the occasion or being spontaneous.

The most important part of "right effort" is to ensure that you find balance; too often, volunteers burn out from the repetition of the tasks they are doing, or from doing too much. If you find yourself feeling resentful or overwhelmed, it's important to act upon your feelings and consult people who support your service practice. An empathic community will realize that you either need a change of activity, some support, or even a break from serving.

"Right effort" also means asking ourselves whether we are serving out of ego or out of a calling to serve. When we first begin to serve, ego may play a major role; to some degree, ego may always play a role, because we must have sufficient ego to believe we have something to offer or we would not be moved to serve at all. Karen Goran, Spiritual Director says, "From a spiritual perspective, true service rests contented in hiddenness. Although it does not fear attention, neither does true service seek out attention. Some say that service is most conducive to the growth of humility, of all the classical spiritual disciplines. It is thought that serving in hiddenness is most transforming, because the ego strives to be noticed, and in this way pride and arrogance are noticed and put to rest. So it requires great strength to notice and resist these natural inclinations."

We can ask ourselves, "Am I making sure people know what I am doing so that I provoke their admiration? Am I doing this to gain the respect of others?" Although others may appreciate our efforts and we are enjoying what we are doing, our service to others is still in its infancy if we are doing it primarily for the positive regard of others. If this is our motivation, it doesn't mean we shouldn't be of service, but rather that we have a ways to go in maturing in our spiritual lives.

I periodically assess the role of service in my life: am I doing enough, am I doing too much? Am I feeling "filled" by the experiences, or "drained" by them? What types of activities stretch me, help me grow? Where can I be of the most help? These are questions that you might ask yourself as you explore "right effort" in serving others in your life.

Effort in serving others develops our ability to determine how much effort we are willing to put into serving our souls as spiritual beings: are we willing to commit to an everyday practice, and how much time will we devote? Are we willing to seek God even when we feel isolated? Are we willing to work through the difficult soul times and not just expect the ecstatic times? When we make sufficient effort to answer these questions, we learn how to navigate and travel meaningfully on the spiritual path.

Meditation

The word meditation often conjures up traditional images of sitting in blissful silence. In the context of serving others, however, meditation takes on a broader, more metaphorical meaning. As Rabbi Steve Robbins says, "Judaism has an intensely meditative tradition built around action, around doing, so that when you take care of the poor, when you clothe people, when you feed them, when you fight for justice, when you work to save the world, when you take care of your family, when you do anything that is of a healing, growing, transformative nature, that is a personal meditative experience. You must enter that experience with that sense of kavannah, of personal spiritual intensity, so that there is nothing you do that is not a prayer, and nothing you do that is not meditative, and nothing you do that is not moral, and nothing you do that doesn't transform the world."

Every time we serve others, we enter the world of intention, devotion and compassion. We can allow ourselves to be distracted and preoccupied with all of the many demands on our lives. Or we can allow ourselves to be fully engaged in our service opportunity. We are called to make an offering of not only our bodies, but our hearts and souls; thus, we are engaged in the world of meditation. The moments when we connect with another person in service, when time disappears and troubles evaporate, when nothing in that moment has meaning except to be present and available, we have entered the world of meditation. Our egos become subdued and our hearts link with the hearts of others.

Sometimes we have this experience of connection without the presence of others. I remember one time during a retreat when I was asked to work outside. The task I had was moving small stones that had been spread on a path from one place to another. It could have been a tedious task, but I found myself fully engaged in studying the rocks, their color, texture, and coolness; the sounds of them tapping against each other as I moved them from place to place. I found myself immersed in the simplicity of the task, aware of the sunshine, the sound of the breeze, the beauty of the landscape. For a while, there were just the rocks and me in each emerging moment.

Being of service reminds us over and over that we serve only this moment, this person, this task, because an event of the past and future can only be present through memory or imagining. When we serve, we give ourselves permission to be fully aware of nothing but *just this*.

Wisdom

I feel awkward talking about wisdom—as if I really knew *anything*. And yet we all are wise in our own ways, and aspire to wisdom all our lives. When we serve others, the culmination of our experiences, our understanding, our learning is transformed into wisdom. We find our teachers everywhere—in the mechanic who works on our cars, our neighbor's child, a client, and the people whom we serve. I often shake my head in wonder at the profound teachings of my friends, my husband, and my family. And I am moved to serve all of them, as they continually serve me by granting me the blessings of their caring and sharing in my life. How does wisdom grow through serving others?

We learn about gratitude. We don't have to search for gratitude; it comes bubbling to the surface, filling our soul space to overflowing, when we realize all the blessings we have in our lives.

We learn about the true meaning of compassion. We move beyond pitying others, which is one way to put ourselves above and separate ourselves from others, and instead we identify with the struggles of others.

We learn to overcome fear. Instead of being contracted and self-centered, we begin to open and expand, connecting with others and understanding that life is more than craving the next new car or promotion.

We learn what it means to allow the Divine to move in our lives and in our relationships with others, and we perceive that although we may feel remote from God, God is ever-present. And we begin to not just believe that, but to *know* that in our lives.

And in serving others, we gain the wisdom to know that wisdom is a gift and an endless journey, and pursuing it, attaining it and honoring it is a central part of our spiritual quest.

What To Do

Serving others can be pursued in many different ways. Sometimes the opportunity to serve walks in the door, and we only have to honor it. The Rev. Kikanza Nuri Robins shared a story about hospitality and serving: "We just hired a choir director, and she's not working full time, and she won't be here often, but she will be here every Sunday. We don't have a lot of space here, and I said to our administrator, we need to find a space for Christine to work, and she said, 'Why? She's not going to be working here that much.' And I said 'She needs to have a desk and she needs to have a cupboard at least, and she needs to have a space that is hers.' And my administrator couldn't understand why, and I said 'It's an act of hospitality; it says to her that we want you here, that you belong here. Look we have made a space for you.'"

Opportunities to serve in our everyday circumstances appear all the time: when I greet the checker in the grocery store; when I offer to give someone a ride with me; when I get my husband a cup of tea. These random acts of kindness enrich our lives and the lives of others, but we gain the most from service when we make a concerted effort to build it into our lives as a regular spiritual practice.

In serving others, ask yourself what you are moved to do: do you want to start out with a familiar or comfortable type of activity, or do you want to do something to stretch yourself? What about helping at a homeless shelter, or a senior citizens' home, or a hospital? Coaching your child's softball team or heading a scout troop? How could you help out at your own church, synagogue, mosque or center? How much time are you willing to give that won't overtax your schedule? Do you like tasks that provide you with a lot of contact with people, or do you want to spend most of the time with only a few people or on your own? The key is finding something that moves your heart, that tests your limits and perceptions of what it means to be a spiritual being.

The Rev. Lois McAfee says this about service:

Overall, serving has come to be for me an experience of partaking in the intersecting of the divine and human dimensions of life in historical time. My serving may help someone hands-on in the immediate situation, or in some collective way, and it's probably a part in God's bigger purposes in the larger mysterious picture in some small way that I may never know. It requires discernment to know what is truly mine to do and what God might be calling someone else to do who is better for the task. Sometimes serving is to stay out of the way. Serving God for others is an incredible privilege. And it is quite enervating. And to receive someone else's service that comes as an answer to a prayer of mine is just as awesome, and just as gratitude-producing.

When we choose to serve others, we are making an offering, a commitment not only to others, but to ourselves and to God. This is your chance to be a budding bodhisattva, to open your heart-mind, and know that being of service is just one more joyous and revealing path to the Divine.

CHAPTER EIGHT

What Questions Does Practice Answer?

It may be hard for you to realize that you can achieve a level that you have never known and that no one near to you has directly experienced. Nevertheless, do not despair of it. This is an important rule. No matter how distant the stage or refined the attribute you hear of, never put it past yourself. Hold it in your heart as a goal and work toward it.
~ RABBI KALONYMUS KALMAN SHAPIRA, *Conscious Community*

I dislike ambiguity; I resent the unknowable; I detest suffering. Why must life be filled with all of these wretched conditions that confuse, frighten and hurt me? When I began a spiritual/religious practice, I didn't know that I was looking for an answer to that question; I only knew that I was looking for answers about life, any answers that would comfort me, help me feel safe, and make life less painful.

I think many of us who are spiritual seekers look to our practices to answer questions that have plagued us for lifetimes, and we hope that in finding these answers, our lives will become more serene and secure. In satisfying these questions, however, we learn that while some questions have answers, others do not; yet we can accept this truth because we also discover that life is abundant with the unknowable and unexplainable. And we learn to find peace in that revelation as well.

Early on I discovered some of my personal "answers" in the Four Noble Truths of Buddhism. The first Noble Truth tells us that life is suffering, or *dukkha*. This word is sometimes defined as living in a constant state of unsatisfactoriness; life is filled with our being unsatisfied, unfulfilled, disappointed, in small as well as significant ways. The second Noble Truth is that there is a cause for this unsatisfactoriness; it is our craving for pleasure and comfort and happiness. The third Noble truth says that we can end our suffering. And the fourth Noble truth says that the Way, or spiritual practice, is the means to get there. For me, the beauty of Buddhism is that it doesn't state that it is the only way or the only path; but if we are to answer some of the most difficult questions of our lives, spirituality is one path to illumination and harmony. So in making the choice to conscientiously pursue a spiritual/religious path, I have committed myself to asking life's questions in a sincere and courageous way, and dedicated myself to a journey that will answer some questions, raise new questions, help me accept that there are unanswerable questions and, most importantly, engage in a dialogue with the Infinite.

In this chapter, I will explore the questions that a spiritual/religious path might help you answer in your everyday life; I will also address the larger-than-life or universal questions whose answers will continue to reveal themselves, as well as describe new questions which may arise; and finally I will share how you can learn to live more peacefully with the unknowable and unexplainable.

Everyday Questions

Before I began a spiritual practice, life was one defensive move after another. I worked hard to protect myself—to protect my reputation, to appear competent, to practice integrity.

Many times when I failed at maintaining this image by making a mistake, disappointing someone or being thoughtless, I felt exposed and frightened. I constantly asked myself, "How can I be perfect? How can I been seen as capable beyond question? How can I make sure that I don't make mistakes?" Gradually I began to realize that the answers that arose from my everyday existence were that there is no perfection, that we are all flawed, and that every time I chastised myself for my frailties or errors, I suffered, and often others did as well.

My spiritual practice led me to these realizations because I was able to quiet my mind, open my heart, allow space for these questions to arise and room for the answers to reveal themselves. When my mind quiets down, I am less inclined to beat up on myself and am less self-centered, and I can ask myself questions such as how can I be more compassionate, how can I best express my love for my husband, my family and my friends? How can I best serve others? As I continue my practice, I have begun to realize that answers are sometimes simple and reveal themselves clearly; at other times, I have begun to comprehend that I have a series of options from which to choose, and I choose what is best for me at that particular time, based on my needs, the needs of others, and the overall situation.

You probably have questions, small and large, simple and complex, that come up in your life every day. As you pursue your spiritual practice, you will find that simple clarity of mind allows for the manifestation of wisdom and compassion. You may also find that the first answers to your questions may raise new questions; you'll want to test your initial answers not only against what feels good or right, but also against the moral foundations of your religious practice: are you upholding the precepts, commandments or laws of your faith? Would this particular answer be the wisest choice, given the circumstances? What good or justice or benefit will come from your decision? What damage might be done? By weighing these additional questions with your initial answers, you will begin to discern the steps you need to take. And you are more likely to make better decisions, because you are acting with your heart, with clarity of mind and with integrity.

Part of my difficulty with every day questions is that, depending on my life circumstances, an answer that seemed appropriate at one time may not seem appropriate at a later time—and this is, in fact, true. Newly emerging answers are an outcome of living my life, which is impermanent and continually evolving. For example, in my team building work, I always strive to be compassionate, and also have a focus on encouraging participants to tell the truth about their thoughts and actions. When I speak the truth about how I see the situation when others are reluctant to do so, I hope that these discussions are revealing and helpful for participants. But facing and acknowledging the truth can also be painful and frightening. I've learned that my direct and forthright style may ultimately not always be the best way to motivate people to explore the truth and communicate honestly and openly with each other. I am now studying other options for creating an environment where participants might be more willing to divulge their thoughts and feelings. I am also exploring my motivations and desires for truth- telling and my role in helping or hindering the sharing process.

So I believe spiritual practice does help answer our every day questions. And the answers may change over time and differ from one person to the next, depending on the particular circumstances, the amount of effort or resources needed, the people involved and the timing of the decision. If you are willing to tune into your own wisdom, give receptive and quiet attention to the answers that may reveal themselves, you will continue to learn about your life.

Universal Questions

As we deepen our spiritual practices, quieting our minds and opening our hearts, we begin to connect with more profound questions and answers. "The real questions are who is God, who am I, what am I doing here, what's my life about, what's my role here, what's my soul mission, what's my soul contract, how do I communicate with God, how do I partner with God, what is God trying to tell me in Torah and Midrash and Talmud, what does God expect of me, what do I expect of God, how should I be in this interrelationship with God, how do I get there from here? These are the questions of the mysteries of the universe, of mystical and spiritual and religious practices." These questions were related to me in a rush of sincerity by Rabbi Wayne Dosick, as he described the questions he understands are part of the deeper questions of life. Although I don't intend to address all these questions, they certainly reflect the complexity and richness of the spiritual life. The Rev. John Jiyu Gage echoed some of the rabbi's sentiments from a different perspective: "To me the basic question being asked by people who are coming to practice is, 'Who am I?' I think the deeper question they are really asking is, 'How can the answer of 'who I am' be fulfilled?' And so their spiritual practice, if it's of any value, is going to bring them to that level of understanding. What that means will be different for different people, and it's going to change at different times during their lives."

In my own life, "who I am" is continually in flux. Even as my body is continually transforming at a cellular level, I am frequently aware that my perspectives, emotions, thoughts, motivations and priorities are also in flux, appearing and disappearing, dominating and retreating. Each time I try to concretely define who this person I call "me" is, I find that the definition is often subject to whether I am joyful or depressed, energized or tired, busy or resting.

A brief five-part definition on "who I am" was given to me by Father John McAndrew, after someone had passed it on to him. It gave me a chuckle, but it certainly offers a perspective on who we are, what our lives are about, and serves to remind us that our issues are universal struggles:

1. Life is unsatisfactoriness.
2. You're not that important.
3. You have no control.
4. You're going to die.
5. It's not about you.

Talk about comeuppance! Whenever I get obsessed about who I am and my importance in the universe, I love to remember that "I'm not that important." What a relief that statement is to me! I'm reminded that there is a whole universe of human beings out there who have to live with the same universal laws as I do, people who wrestle with the same life issues, and whose existence reminds me that rather than feeling isolated, we are all sharing this lifetime, together.

Another one of the universal questions we try to answer is, "Why am I here?" This question is also one that can be studied, contemplated and nurtured through spiritual practice. As you evolve in your ability to understand the nature of your life, your role in this life comes into focus; your purpose becomes better defined and more precious to you. As you go deeper into exploring the nature of your purpose, you become more committed to sharing your gifts and talents with others. At this point, some of your greatest rewards and satisfactions will come not just from developing spiritually on your own, but from sharing your love, compassion and understanding by serving others. Service to others is not done out of obligation, but out of a desire to help others appreciate their own lives.

I love to learn. But if I can't find ways to express my learning and gifts in everyday life, then life is like watering a plot of land that has no seeds. Instead of letting the land lie fallow, I practice my spiritual experiences to grow lush gardens that I can harvest and share with others. Whether it's encouraging my husband when he's down, guiding a client who's in distress, or listening to a friend who needs an empathic ear—all these are opportunities that answer my question, over and over again, of why I am here.

Perhaps the greatest question of all is, who or what is God? For me, it is impossible to define God, because each time I try to do it, I am confined by the limitations of my own mind, which cannot begin to comprehend what God is. But rather than try to set limits to my understanding of God or the universal spirit, through my spiritual practice I can open myself up to the endless opportunities for experiencing God. I believe that God is omnipresent, unfathomable and limitless. At the same time, I can paradoxically believe that God's love and wisdom are available, accessible and unwavering. Although I wish my human, everyday logic could explain how God operates, I become humble in my realization that there is no way to comprehend the mind of God. Rather than having to constrict and circumscribe my perceptions of God, my potential experiences of the Infinite are boundless and open to endless possibility. I realize that faith and commitment are my lifeline to God, and I no longer need to define the indefinable or explain the inexplicable. I can simply live the life of Spirit.

New Questions

A spiritual life constantly raises new questions. When you pursue a spiritual practice, you naturally cultivate an environment for the manifestation of both wisdom and compassion. As a spiritual seeker, you ceaselessly aspire to understand the nature of your life which is ongoingly changing and maturing. And your process for finding answers—whether they are answers you desire or that the universe calls for you to know—is asking new questions.

A spiritual life provides not only a belief system for leading a life of principle and truth; it also challenges you to understand the nature of principle and truth and how you can live them out in your every day life. Spirit does not ask you only to follow rules blindly and to pursue the path obediently; it stimulates you to delve into the very foundations of truth, to grasp the meaning behind your practice, to perceive the heart of joy and the roots of suffering. As your practice deepens, you begin to see each new question, not as one more trial to overcome, but as a stimulus and tool for immersing yourself in the complexities of life with curiosity and equanimity, and for discovering how to lead a life of goodness and truth. You also slowly begin to realize that, although you may be inspired to learn all that there is to know about the spiritual life, there are some questions that you may never be able to answer.

Living with the Unknowable

"Religion raises more questions than it gives answers, but it also allows you to become more comfortable with the questions." So says the Rev. Kikanza Nuri Robins. One outcome of leading a life of spirit is that life transforms from an existence of contraction, protection and confinement, to one of spaciousness, openness and receptivity. My own experience has been that instead of having to define clearly every aspect of my existence, I recognize the freedom of opening to learning and possibilities. I chuckle at the messiness of ambiguity, and breathe more easily within the expansiveness of "not knowing."

The paradox of spiritual practice is that you pursue some questions knowing that they may never be fully answered, and yet hope that you can glimpse, even for a moment, the clarity, truth and meaning of existence. You pursue the answers to the unknowable questions, not with frustration or disappointment, but with curiosity and delight. You realize that there is great value not just in finding answers, but in the spiritual journey itself. You learn how to expand your awareness, investigate without judgment, and accept the answers or the absence of answers with patience and a willingness to surrender to the ineffable.

So spiritual practice answers some questions, presents us with new questions and helps us exist peacefully with the knowledge that there are some questions that we may never answer. Living a life of spirit helps us live with, and appreciate, this truth.

CHAPTER NINE

How Does Practice
Change Your Life?

"The movement from loneliness to solitude is a movement by which we reach out to our innermost being to find there our great healing powers, not as a unique property to be defended but as a gift to be shared with all human beings." ~ Henri Nouwen *Reaching Out*

Before I even began to work on this chapter, I was filled with trepidation; what in the world could I, a novice on the religious/spiritual path, say about how spiritual practice transforms one's life? After postponing the writing on this chapter for weeks, I finally followed the procedure I'd used for previous chapters: I went back to the heartfelt and descriptive narratives of the people I'd interviewed. I realized after reading my notes extensively that while the interviewees shared the general indicators of transformation, most of them also struggled with describing the *experience* of transformation. Now I was really nervous; if they firmly believed in transformation, but had difficulty describing it, how in the world would I be able to do it? I finally realized that I had only one choice: I would have to describe the struggles, realizations and process of transformation from my own experience and understanding.

I believe that transformation is so difficult to describe because it is not an external, objective or rational process; it is a deeply personal, sometimes painful, evolutionary process—at least for me. Transformation is not about changing into someone other than who I am; it's about becoming more authentically who I am. For some people, transformation is sudden, powerful and overwhelming; for others, including myself, transformation has been an evolving and gradual process. Transformation isn't about my getting somewhere or becoming a perfected human being; it isn't about my living a life of eternal equanimity and peace; it isn't about escaping the suffering of life or experiencing only gladness and enjoyment. Instead, transformation is about the dropping away of the false selves, about seeing one's life more clearly, about piercing the curtain of delusive thought, and appreciating both the simplicity and complexities of life.

Transformation is about relating to life where I am not sitting on the banks of the stream of existence, but I am immersed in the stream. I am the bouncing current, the wetness of the water and the roughness of the rocks. I am the dancing fish and the misty spray that hangs like a curtain, waiting to open. I am both a witness of the stream from every vantage point and I *am* the stream as it meanders, brushes the banks, touches the rocks and relentlessly pursues its path. For me, transformation is not seeing myself as only one part of the stream, but aspiring to see myself as all of it, never separate from it. It is about celebrating life with all that it has to offer, without trying to pick and choose what I like or don't like, or what pleases me or dissatisfies me. It is a lifelong process, and it is not about transcending human existence, but about becoming as authentically and compassionately human as I can.

In living a religious/spiritual life, I have found that life has never been richer. As I've gone deeper and deeper into my religious/spiritual practice, I intuitively know that there is something essential, mysterious and transcendent at the core of my being, yet there is simultaneously a sense of being at one, at home, at peace with the immanent aspects of divinity. This paradox of essence and impermanence, transcendence and immanence, Self and no-self is perhaps the ultimate spiritual mystery that cannot be spoken of directly but is at the heart of the spiritual life. I also know the wisdom and compassion that continue to evolve and expand within me along the way will ultimately make the journey worthwhile.

In this chapter I will relate the cumulative and transformative effects of leading a religious/spiritual life. I will talk about (1) creating space; (2) witnessing your life; (3) experiencing wholeness; (4) finding intimacy with life; and (5) discovering meaning. In a sense all of these occur interdependently and simultaneously; they are like a spiral that descends into the innermost recesses of our being, yet simultaneously ascends into the expansiveness of all of existence. Their evolution is both intensely personal and yet limitless in their impact. And they have all been the continually emerging and maturing aspects of my living a life of Spirit.

Creating Space

In experiencing transformation, my life has evolved as if I were moving from a shoe box to living in a home; I know that there is even much more of life beyond the limits of a home, but for me, that movement from darkness to spaciousness has been profound. The shoe box of my life was one of restriction and severe limitations; there was little room for others, no opportunities for authentic expansion and exploration. It was a life of emotional and spiritual subsistence. Since there was little room for others or for my own movement, I lived under the illusion that I was protected and safe. Those who dared to enter my shoe box had to pass severe tests of acknowledging my fear, demonstrating their patience and proving their love for me.

As time passed, and my religious/spiritual practice matured, I gradually removed the lid of the shoe box and peeked out. I saw there was light on the other side, room to move around and explore. As I climbed out of the shoe box, I began to breathe more easily, felt a little less frightened. I began to take risks in relationships, open to the heartfelt advances of others, and was moved to return their efforts. For a while, I continued to stand by the shoe box, holding on to its cave-like security, trying to decide if I really wanted to relinquish its isolation and comfort. What I didn't realize was that once I stepped out of the shoe box, I could never return: as I emerged from the shoe box, I had grasped the hand of Spirit, and my heart would not allow me to let it go.

Over time, I have found that although fear still sometimes infuses my life, I am beginning to rejoice in the freedom of living a life of Spirit. I feel liberated from many aspects of my fear, and often feel the spaciousness of opportunities and the multitude of choices I have for seeing my life as rewarding and precious. When I become angry or frustrated, I am able to let go of the anger and frustration sooner; I am able more often to relate to my emotions rather than feel over-powered by them; I am more willing to forgive others and forgive myself when things don't go my way. When I feel hurt or disappointed by others, I am more inclined to see their points of view, often seeing my role in events and relationships.

As I let go more and more often of my need to have people meet my expectations, I become more curious about the nature of my rela-tionship with others and more willing to explore relating in totally different ways; letting go has become a state of receptivity, rather than an effort to overcome fear. At times I have even experienced surren-dering to that *which is*: I recognize that I have no power to change certain things, and I submit to the unavoidable. Although this deci-sion can be difficult and fraught with disappointment, it is also a com-mitment to embrace the inevitable.

When I take a deep breath now, it isn't necessarily just a sign of resignation; more often, it is an acknowledgment of this moment, with its surprises, ordinariness, sadness or joy. It punctuates the state of my being present, of consciousness and awareness. As constriction and guardedness dissolve, spaciousness and flexibility expand—and Spirit grows.

Witnessing Your Life

In the everyday scheme of things, it's not readily apparent that trans-formation is taking place. Instead, it is easy for me to become engulfed in the chaos of life. At times I feel baffled, overwhelmed, overpowered and disoriented by the events of my life that go whizzing past. I feel swept along by the choices of others, out of control and sometimes powerless to live my life differently. As more space is created for understanding my life, however, a dedicated life practice of religion and spirit have allowed me to step back and observe my life with more clarity, acceptance and equanimity.

In becoming a witness to my life, I've begun to identify my patterns for coping with life. Some of those patterns are productive, others are not; and they are all my life. In recognizing that I sometimes take unproductive actions, I make the effort to simply witness the action that represents a lifetime pattern, rather than punish myself for what I have done. I just notice my attitudes and preferences from a place of curiosity, and instead of pouring my energy into judging myself a good or bad person, I guide my energy into compassion for myself and the exploration of other options: what might I do differently next time? How might I respond more productively or compassionately? How might I be more helpful to myself and others involved? What is it that I'm wanting? Is that something I can have? What are my underlying feelings and am I willing to experience the full range of emotions that have been triggered? Am I willing to see the situation from other perspectives?

As time goes on, I have begun to develop the capacity to notice that there is nothing concrete or objective about my perceptions of my life. As my spiritual practice has evolved, I have begun to notice my preference to blame others and defend myself; I observe my reactions and step back for a moment to experience my emotions and study my thoughts: am I wanting to feel safe, look good? Am I wishing to punish the other person? Does the other person have a perspective that I might want to explore? What do I gain through blaming others and defending myself? What do I lose? As I delve into the ways that I perceive and experience my life, I begin to see the filters that distort my perception of reality. I realize that as life unfolds, I develop stories in my mind that create an illusion of meaning as well as twisting the truth. Much of my effort to maintain my desire for life to be orderly and sane only creates barriers and dissension between myself and others, who see and experience life differently.

The more I witness my life, the more I've begun to realize how much effort I expend in creating an image of myself, to satisfy my own need for safety and to impress others. In creating this image, I discourage others from knowing me; my actions are ego-based and inauthentic, my motivations are suspect. As I continue to witness my behavior, I discover opportunities to respond to life more genuinely. I realize there is no way to be completely safe, and I begin to reveal who I am, warts and all. Instead of acting defensively, I reach out to nurture relationships, express compassion, and support the lives of others. I experience God's intervention, particularly when I am awake enough to recognize the choices I can make that enhance, rather than damage relationships. In recognizing that I can engage life in many ways, and that the world keeps spinning even when I make a mistake or am unsuccessful, I begin to experience self-acceptance.

Ultimately in living a life of Spirit, my quest is to be a witness to the entirety of my life, my strengths and limitations, and to live my life with integrity from a place of love and understanding. As I live a life of Spirit and receive guidance from the Infinite, I become more and more the witness of who I am, and more accepting of all that I am.

Experiencing Wholeness

I have had my share of hurts—not getting enough of one thing, getting too much of another. In many instances I went through life feeling wounded and entitled, and judged those with whom I was in relationship by how much they might potentially hurt or betray me. It's not that I didn't encounter joy and light in my life, but I wanted to guarantee that nothing would interfere with those positive experiences. I wanted to feel safe. I wanted to be immune from hurt. I wanted to be in control.

One of my hopes in pursuing a religious/spiritual life was that I might find a process that would free me from anguish; that I would eventually be able to move through personal calamities with calmness and aplomb. In some ways I do approach events with a more balanced perspective; I'm less reactive and more inquisitive, more willing to explore another person's point of view. From another perspective, though, I'm also discovering how to experience all of my life more deeply; even though anguish and hurt can still pierce my heart and take my breath away, joy is now able to lift me to the clouds and call me to sing to the stars. What Spirit is teaching me is to embrace all of my life, including the hurts and the blessings. In the process of thoroughly embracing all that I experience, I have learned that I will survive the ups and downs, and that on the other side of grief and disillusionment are awareness and self-acceptance.

As I'm learning to accept myself, the wounds in my life have begun to heal. I've asked forgiveness from some of those whom I realize I have hurt, intentionally or not. Even more, I have made the effort to forgive myself for the damage I have done, for the hurts I have inflicted, for the separateness I have created. As I take these steps, I have felt my heart mend, my sadness lessen, and my regrets fade. I cannot change the past; I can only mend and heal the present.

At first I felt accused unfairly—how could she make me into such a terrible person! I spent weeks in imaginary conversations, defending myself and accusing her of betraying our relationship. As the weeks passed, my resolve to confront her began to dissolve. Although I realized she did have a role in our troubled relationship, I also acknowledged that I had done damage. I had given unsolicited advice; I had spoken truths that she didn't want to hear; I had unconsciously belittled and criticized her, hoping "the truth" would get through to her. And I had, for now, lost her.

In all these years, she had never told me her feelings about me. I can only guess why. I have extended an invitation to her, to tell me all the things she was never willing or able to tell me. I will not attack her; she will not have to defend herself. I only want to create a safe place. I will only listen. Be present. Hear her truth.

Transformation calls to me to accept, as best I can, whatever life has to offer. As I immerse myself in life's happenings, fear lessens and love grows. In the process of fully experiencing life, I invite the Infinite One to heal my wounds, to comfort me, and to make me whole.

Finding Intimacy with Life

As the transformation process expands and space is created, as self-acceptance grows and healing manifests, I have continued to emerge from isolation and become more intimate with my life. This intimacy has evolved in my personal relationships, in my acknowledgment of my own rich life, and in my relationship with God.

She's called to tell me about a project she is working on; it's quite wonderful to see someone her age with so much talent, curiosity and zest for life. I love to be around her because she gives me hope that my senior years will be productive, engaging and full of vigor. We finish talking and say good-bye. A few minutes later the telephone rings again, and she has called back to apologize for something she felt she didn't express clearly the night before. I'm puzzled about her concern, and she proceeds to share her admiration for me and all that I am doing. I am embarrassed and moved. I tell her I feel blessed, and thank her for the gift of her words; I remind her that friends like her move me and motivate me to do what I do. What would I do without the love and support of my friends?

As I have begun to develop closer relationships with people in my life, I have learned that we have more in common than our interests, goals and desires; we also share similar concerns about intimacy, the same fears, the same questions: what does it mean to be close to another person? What kinds of risks am I willing to take to know others, and to be known? What things can I say or do that will create bridges rather than barriers in my relationships? How can we all feel less fearful as we learn and grow together?

In addition to nurturing more intimate personal relationships, I have become more intimate with myself. For the first couple of years after moving back to California, I remember telling people that I couldn't understand my good fortune: I found work projects right away; professional people to affiliate with; new friends. Why was I so blessed? What did it mean that I was so fortunate? One day I voiced my bewilderment to a friend in Colorado about how well life was going, and she said, "Oh, I stopped asking those kinds of questions long ago. I just feel appreciation." Her words penetrated my resistance to accepting and rejoicing in my life. Somehow I was feeling that I wasn't deserving; that other people were more deserving of the happiness and contentment I was experiencing. I felt distant from my own joy, my own success, my own life. Her words reminded me that there is no way to anticipate grace. When we receive the gifts of friendship, success and happiness, we only need to give thanks, and share our wealth with others.

Now I try to notice when I discount or try to rationalize my life. When I get caught up in analyzing, doubting, and separating myself from my life experience, I try to shift my perspective. If nothing else, I take a moment of silence to simply say "thank you—Baruch HaShem—thank you, God" for the gifts of my life. Thank you for a husband who loves and supports me. Thank you for friends who encourage and care for me. Thank you for clients and colleagues who work with me and respect me. Thank you for work that fulfills and challenges me. Thank you for the gifts of understanding, awareness and compassion. Thank you for bringing beauty and happiness into my life. Thank you for gracing my life.

Intimacy with my life also is about being more and more willing to accept those things I cannot change. It means recognizing that even when difficult, frustrating or hurtful events occur that they, too, are my life. Learning to work with, study and embrace those times when life doesn't seem fair has been a valuable part of my journey. Instead of running from conflict or attacking it, I'm now trying to examine it and engage in it in a way that is meaningful and sincere. Although I can't imagine that difficult times will ever be easy to face, they have frequently become less traumatic for me. I approach them with less anxiety and more curiosity. I rush to judgment less often and hold open the possibility of exploration and dialogue with others. When I can't change the situation, I am sometimes able to accept the truth, and allow myself to experience sadness and letting go. And in experiencing sadness, that, too, is an element of my life that I can welcome and investigate. The difficulties, the sadness, the fear, the curiosity beckon to me to know them and engage them. All this, just this, is my life.

Discovering Meaning

I can tell that he is very frightened. I am here to interview him for a workshop, but he has been hostile from the moment he entered the room. I've been told that he might refuse to talk to me, but in spite of his reluctance to engage, we have discovered that we have a lot in common in just five minutes of conversation. Suddenly, in talking about the workshop, I have triggered something in him; he becomes enraged, tells me forcefully that "this conversation is over," and walks out of the room. I am stunned. What did I say? What did I trigger in him? What was he experiencing? Rather than being angry, I am deeply moved by how frightened he is, and concerned that I have unintentionally contributed to some hidden emotional pain. An hour later, after the next interview, he slips into the room; I find myself momentarily frightened, wondering about his potential rage. But he has only come in to apologize. I tell him I am sorry, too. I invite him to set up another time to talk, and tell him I will call to see if he's willing. Later I leave a message on his voice mail. He doesn't return my call. And it's okay.

Transformation, at its most profound level for me, has been about exploring, discovering and learning why I am here and how I can contribute. In my work, I want more than anything to create a safe place where other people can explore their lives in search of meaning. I want to be able to be present to their pain, their rage, their anxiety, their futility, their reluctance; I want them to know there is hope on the other side of despair; I want them to know that life, in and of itself, is rich and abundant; I want them to know that they, too, can find fulfillment in life, if they are willing to do the work.

I try to remind myself that I can best help when I am welcome. To give opinions to people who are not interested or open to another point of view only alienates them and damages the relationships. It means that when I see others taking a path that may hurt them, I must learn to live with my own emotions of sadness and fear for them; my reluctance to experience painful emotions about their choices does not justify my intruding upon the lives of others. I have also learned that when I own my feelings and share them with another person (my concern, my fear, my sadness) as well as express another point of view, I sometimes am more easily heard; I am coming less from a place of judgment and more from a place of concern and caring. Then my thoughts are more likely to have meaning. Even then, I need to be very clear on whether I am injecting myself into people's situations for their sakes—or for mine. If it's for my own benefit (to look good, to be right, to be superior or condescending), I'm not helping them.

When people are willing to come to the place where they are ready to pursue a life of meaning, I want to be able to reflect their feelings, understand their dilemmas, empathize with their hurting, and assist them in their journey. These interactions with others are the opportunities that give my life meaning, that have taught me what it means to be a companion to others, to help others, to know compassion and love.

This area of my life—how and when to serve—has actually become a spiritual practice for me. The exploration of my motivations, the understanding of others' needs and expectations, figuring out how I can be most helpful—through listening or giving input or both—this has become my latest mission. The very act of exploring these elements makes helping others a complex, challenging and meaningful experience. It is not something I practice lightly. I have a gift to offer to others, but it is only a gift if it is welcome and helpful. To be able to investigate the significance of service and how best to provide it has engaged me in life in a more profound, loving and lively way. It has made me more mindful of the distress of others; it has created empathy and connection; it has helped me observe and appreciate my relationship with others. It has been the form and substance of my religious and spiritual path. It has given my life meaning.

Transformation is an ongoing process that permeates everyday life. It brings me joy and love. It brings me frustration and disappointment.

But most of all, in a way that no other life experience can provide, it vastly enriches my life. I am awed by it. I am moved by it. I am incredibly grateful for the opportunity to live life with less fear and more love, to mature in my relationships with others and to know what it means to have the Infinite be the essence of my life. That is what it means to transform.

CHAPTER TEN

How Do You Create
Your Own Path?

Seen through the eyes of faith, religion's future is secure. As long as there are human beings, there will be religion for the sufficient reason that the self is a theomorphic creature—one whose morphe (form) is theos— God encased within it. Having been created in the imago Dei, the image of God, all human beings have a God-shaped vacuum built into their hearts. Since nature abhors a vacuum, people keep trying to fill the one inside them. Searching for an image of the divine that will fit, they paw over various options as if they were pieces of a jigsaw puzzle, matching them successively to the gaping hole at the puzzle's center . . . they keep doing this until the right "piece" is found. When it slips into place, life's jigsaw puzzle is solved. ~ Huston Smith, *Why Religion Matters.*

I've related to you some of the possibilities of what a religious/spiritual path can look like. You've read the inspirations, beliefs and convictions of those who embrace both mainstream and contemporary religions as well as personal spiritual practices. Perhaps now you're moved to develop a more deeply spiritual life for yourself, but you don't know which way to turn, where to go, or what step to take next. Perhaps you're anxious; or you may be fearful of what it means to commit to a religious/spiritual life. You may feel excited about embarking on an adventure, or you may be peering down the depths of the spiritual path with some reserve and trepidation. Or you may simply be curious. Wherever you may be, I'd like to offer some options and suggestions for you to consider for getting started on your own unique spiritual path.

A Roadmap to the Spiritual Path

One of the best ways to begin the development of your own spiritual path is to develop a roadmap for the journey. By designing a roadmap to create a spiritual path, you will be able to pursue a more profound exploration to determine which religious practices are most congruent with your own life view, and identify the spiritual practices that work best for you.

Investigating the possibilities for your own path can be a complex and lengthy process. Without some type of map, you may find yourself easily becoming frustrated and confused by the wealth of spiritual opportunities available to you. With a map, you will be able to ascertain the paths to look into, the factors that are important to you, and the practices that connect you with Spirit and the universal. The map doesn't have to include a lot of detail or analysis, but will help you chart the course of your exploration, document your findings in a simple manner, and assist you in determining the journey that speaks best to your heart and soul.

This chapter focuses on how to investigate both communal and personal practices, as well as seek the assistance of a spiritual guide. You may have difficulty deciding whether to begin your spiritual journey by associating with a religious community, by creating your own personal spiritual practices, or by doing both at the same time. My goal is to help you begin your journey precisely where you are right now, mentally, physically, emotionally and spiritually, whether you are with, or want to be with, a community, or you want to journey on your own.

Your travel through the communal opportunities can include the benefits of reading about and experiencing participation in community. In studying personal practices, I'll describe how to begin developing your own practices and how to get support from others. Finally, a spiritual guide can provide some direction if you get stuck in the early stages of clarifying your needs and expectations for the spiritual life.

Starting with Community

If you already have a personal spiritual practice, or don't know where to begin your inquiry regarding religious community, the first landmark on your spiritual roadmap may be reading, a wonderful way to inquire, learn and scrutinize the many religious practices available to you.

By reading, you will survey a wide range of ideas, belief systems, and values of many of the religions that are practiced. (See Appendix 3) As you read, notice what ideas speak not only to your head, but also to your heart. Rather than looking at each religion with a judgmental eye, study it with curiosity and wonder; think about whether it makes sense to you and brings you closer to the body of Spirit. Remember that no religion will meet all your needs perfectly; as you begin your quest, you are only looking at the overall "systems": the themes of particular religious practices, the views and doctrines that are held.

In addition to reading, the next milestone on your roadmap may be studying and engaging with religious communities and their various personalities and practices. If you grew up with a particular tradition, and simply abandoned it out of a lack of connection or interest, but agreed with the overall belief system, you might begin there. Give some thought to what was missing from the religious practice or community you were involved in, and how you might find a community that has similar beliefs, but engages in ways that have meaning and purpose for you.

If you were raised without a formal religion, or are unwilling to participate in the religion in which you were raised, think specifically about your expectations from a religious community:

- Would you like to participate in a large or small community?

- Are you interested in participating in small group activities where it's often easier to get to know people?

- If your answer is yes, what kind of small group activities are you interested in? Prayer groups? Meditation groups? Social groups? Social action groups? Family-oriented groups? Twelve-step programs?

- How do you feel about ritual? Do you like a simple, contemporary and informal service, or do you prefer a traditional form with ritual and ancient prayer?

- Do you prefer worship in English or do you enjoy chanting and singing in other languages as well?

- What kind of a religious leader are you looking for? Do you want someone who teaches and supports personal spiritual practices?

- Is it important for the spiritual leader to be charismatic? Social action-oriented? Actively involved with community activities?

If you are uncertain about any of these questions, explore communities that represent a wide variety of offerings; this approach can be not only fun, but will probably be one of the most practical ways for you to determine the type of community that best fits your temperament and expectations.

Once you have an idea of what you are looking for in a community, ask friends or colleagues about their religious communities. Ask them about the belief systems and values; what do they like and not like about the communities in which they're involved; do these communities meet the profiles you are interested in. If you like what you hear, ask if you might attend services with them. If you feel that you've connected with the form and substance of the services, you may then find out more about the community; you can have additional discussions with the person who brought you as a guest, and you might even want to arrange an appointment with the religious leader of the community. Some communities welcome guests to their small group activities as well; at these meetings and get-togethers you will have the opportunity to become better acquainted and get a sense of the people who are involved.

When I first joined the Three Treasures Zen Community, I was immediately drawn to many aspects of the community. I had already been involved with Zen for three years, so I knew a lot about my preferences for community and practice. I learned that this community was, in many respects, a traditional Zen community, but that they were inclusive of people who were not interested in formal and traditional Zen practices. The community itself was diverse, from teen-agers to people in their 80s. Retreats were offered on a regular basis, and ranged from informal (without formal services or traditional eating practices) to the traditional with formal clothing, services, *oryoki* (ceremonial form of eating meals in silence) and chanting. From my first visit, people were warm and engaging, the teachers were sincere and supportive and the membership was small. I loved the creativity, inclusiveness and intimacy of the community, and knew it was a good match for me.

Even though I sensed the warmth of the community, I knew I also had to extend myself to get to know people and to become comfortable with everyone. Gradually I made a point of introducing myself to people I didn't know. I participated in task groups and social activities. I tried to attend sitting meditation every week to become more familiar with the more formal practices that I hadn't yet learned and to have time to become better acquainted with everyone. I became a member of the Board of Directors. I volunteered to help where I could. (Before you start to cringe at the thought of this level of involvement, remember that the amount and type of involvement is up to you. The fact is that the more involved you become, the more intimate you can become with the community.)

I'm not saying that I selected the perfect community, either. There are times when I become frustrated with someone or impatient, or am disappointed. There are some people that I've become friends with, others with whom I may only have our Zen practice in common. I can honestly say that although I may not be friends with everyone, I have come to appreciate everyone with whom I've become acquainted in the community. Every person contributes in his or her own, special way.

As you visit communities, attend more than once those that seem to have potential; your first visit is bound to be somewhat superficial, and succeeding visits will provide you with a more in-depth perspective of the community. As you appraise the community, be discriminating but not overly critical, particularly if you have had unpleasant experiences with religious communities in the past. Look for things that reflect the potential and opportunities that the community offers, rather than criticizing it for not offering everything. You might also think about not only what the community offers you, but what you might have to offer to the community; offering our gifts is one way of feeling welcomed and included.

Finally, you might want to keep a journal of your experiences. You can do this by formally recording your impressions, or you can keep an informal description of what worked for you in each exposure to a community, and what didn't. By keeping a journal, you will start to notice patterns that reflect the offerings of a community that you value, and the aspects of community that are not as important. These observations will help you refine and clarify your expectations of a religious community, and move you along your spiritual path.

Starting with Personal Practice

If the idea of investigating religious communities makes you uneasy, or if you are already affiliated with a religious community, the next leg of your spiritual roadmap can be examining the various kinds of personal spiritual practices. In Chapter 4 we looked at many kinds of spiritual practices, including receptive practices, which are usually done quietly and alone, and active practices that offer movement and sometimes interaction with others. When trying to decide which practices to try, always "start where you are." Don't try practices that seem overly difficult or that frustrate you.

As I've said earlier in this book, start slowly and simply. Limit the number of practices that you select, preferably starting with one. Decide what draws you to a personal practice: do you look forward to simply being still, slowing down, opening up to what is present? Are you attracted to a dynamic practice that allows you sing or dance or funnel your energy into connecting with Spirit? Choose a reasonable amount of time to spend on personal practice, and choose a time of day when you are least likely to be interrupted. Since this type of practice may be new for you, I suggest you give yourself time to decide whether it works for you or not; a one-month trial period will help you decide. If one month seems too long, set a time period that is reasonable for you and stick with it. Many people give up on personal practices because they've set unrealistic goals, get discouraged or become overly critical of their ability to practice regularly, and give up. As lofty as personal practice may sound, I try to treat it like brushing my teeth: I don't ask myself in the morning and at night whether I should brush my teeth on a particular day—I just do it. When you build practice into a regular part of your daily routine, you actually miss doing it if something unavoidable interferes.

One way to sustain a personal practice is to find other people who will practice with you. You don't necessarily have to have people from the same religious practice, as long as you are open to sharing ideas from all the religions involved. Before I became active with Three Treasures Zen Community, I was part of a sitting group that met once a week. At first we met in my office conference room; then we moved to a member's home. We tried to make time to visit informally before and after our sitting time. Another friend formed a small weekly sitting group that he and his wife hosted. They would meditate for two, thirty-minute periods separated by walking meditation, and then would discuss a reading which was distributed in advance to participants. By meeting once a week in both groups, we supported each others' practices and also got better acquainted through discussion.

Regardless of how you decide to develop your own personal practice, it is a wonderful way to feel connected—to Spirit, to the universe, to your life. Making time just for this type of intimacy creates a depth to religious/spiritual practices that is rewarding and fulfilling. If you just can't seem to decide which direction to follow, whether it is regarding your personal practice or religious community, a spiritual guide may be the answer.

Starting with a Spiritual Guide

You want to do *something* but you just don't know where to start; you may consider a spiritual guide to help you create your spiritual roadmap. A spiritual guide is trained to help you clarify where you are spiritually, and what steps you might take to move forward.

As explained in Chapter 6, spiritual guides can be found in all kinds of places. Again, you might ask trusted friends and family if there is a member of the clergy whom they admire and trust; most clergy have received some training in counseling. There are also Christian clergy of many denominations who have participated in the in-depth and comprehensive training in spiritual direction provided by the Roman Catholic church. This program is specifically designed to train people who want to provide spiritual direction to seekers. Many eastern religions, including Zen Buddhism, provide paths for seekers who want to be spiritual teachers; many of these practices center on the student-teacher relationship as an important aspect of spiritual development. Appendix 2 also lists organizations that train and provide spiritual directors.

Qualified spiritual guides will not tell you what to do; instead, they intend to guide you through the confusion, resistance or inertia you may be experiencing regarding your pursuing your spiritual journey. They can provide resources, reading materials and options to help you get unstuck as you try to determine what it means to lead a spiritual life. Once you reach some clarity on the direction you might pursue, you'll be better equipped to determine whether your next step is to engage in community, develop a personal practice or both.

Whether you know it or not, if you've come this far, you have already begun your personal spiritual journey. Who knows what lies ahead? If you continue to pursue this path, you will find that the journey is rich beyond measure, mysterious beyond imagination, and fulfilling beyond your spiritual hopes and dreams. It will be challenging, engaging, maturing and enlightening. It will take you down paths you've never seen before. And it will connect you with Spirit and the universe in a way that no other practice can. Welcome and best wishes on your own unique spiritual journey!

List of Interviewees

Swami Atmavidyananda, treasurer, Vedanta Society of Southern California

Fr. Wilfredo Benitez, spiritual leader of St. Anselm's of Canterbury Episcopal Church

The Rev. Margie Clark, spiritual leader of the Seal Beach Church of Religious Science

Charlotte Cleghorn, Episcopal priest and spiritual director

Karen Goran, Presbyterian and member of the Episcopal Church of the Messiah, independent spiritual director and leader of a meditation group

Sister Jane DeLisle, executive director of the Center for Spiritual Development

Rabbi Wayne Dosick, spiritual leader of The Elijah Minyan

Bishop Murray D. Finck, Pacific Synod, Evangelical Lutheran Church in America

Anne Seisen Saunders, Sensei, Sweetwater Zen Center

The Rev. John Gage, teacher, Three Treasures Zen Community

Jan Hoffman, Quaker, practitioner and speaker

Fr. Brad Karelius, spiritual leader of the Episcopal Church of the Messiah

Linda Klassen, Protestant, counselor in a missionary organization

Kay Lindahl, director for the Alliance for Spiritual Community

Pastor Craig Lockwood, Vineyard Christian Fellowship

The Rev. Lois McAffee, unaffiliated spiritual director (United Methodist Church)

Nicolee Jikyo McMahon, Sensei, spiritual leader of Three Treasures Zen Community

Rabbi Jonathan Omer-Man, spiritual leader and Rabbi Emeritus of the Metivta Center

Pastor Van Pewthers, Vineyard Christian Fellowship

The Rev. Preston Price, spiritual leader of the United Methodist Church, Garden Grove and spiritual director

Rabbi Steve Robbins, spiritual leader of Temple N'vay Shalom

Dr. Kikanza Nuri Robins, Presbyterian minister

Swami Sarvadevananda, assistant minister, Vedanta Society of Southern California

Dr. Muzammil Siddiqi, director of the Islamic Society of Orange County

Mary Strouse, member of St. Polycarp's Catholic Church

The Venerable Chon Thanh, Buddhist spiritual leader of Lien Hoan Temple

Organizational Resources*

Buddhism

American Buddhist Congress. Website: www.wgn.net

Lien Hoa Temple Temple, 9561 Bixby Ave., Garden Grove, CA 92841. Phone: (714) 636-7725

Zen Mountain Center, P.O. Box 43, Mountain Center, CA 92561, Phone: (909) 659-5272. Website: www.zmc.org

Sweetwater Zen Center, 2727 Highland Ave., National City, CA 91950. Phone: (619) 477-0390. E-mail: Sweetwater@swzc.org

Three Treasures Zen Community, P.O. Box 754, Del Mar, CA 92014. Phone: (760) 745-4249. Website: www.ttzc.org

Wake Up Opening Page/Zen Mountain Monastery, New York. Website: www.zen-mtn.org

Unified Buddhist Church (founded by Zen monk Thich Nhat Hanh). Website: www.plumvillage.org

Catholic Church

St. Angela Merici Church, 585 S. Walnut Ave., Brea, CA 92821. Phone: (714) 529-1821

Catholic Information Center on Internet. Website: www.catholic.net

Catholic Information Network. Website: www.catholicity.com

St. John Newmann Church, 5101 Alton Parkway, Irvine, CA 92714. Phone: (714) 559-4006

---

* A partial listing of organizations featured in this book plus contact information for national offices of varoius religious communities.

Episcopal Church

Anglican Church in America. Website: www.acahome.org

Episcopal Church Center. 815 2nd Ave., New York, New York 10017. Phone: (800) 334-7626. Website: www.ecusa.anglican.org

Episcopal Church, Diocese of Los Angeles, 840 Echo Park Ave., P.O. Box 512164, Los Angeles, CA 90051-0164. Phone: (213) 482-2040. Website: www.ladiocese.org

Episcopal Church of the Messiah, 614 N. Bush St. Santa Ana, CA 92701. Phone: (714) 543-9389

Grace Cathedral (includes walking labyrinth), 1100 California St., San Francisco, CA 94108. Phone: (415) 749-6300. Website: www.gracecathedral.org

St. Anselm's Episcopal Church (includes walking labyrinth), 13091 Galway St., Garden Grove, CA 92844. Phone: (714) 537-0604

Quakers

Friends General Conference, 1216 Arch St., 2B, Philadelphia, PA 19107. Phone: (800) 966-4556. E-mail: fgc@fgc.quaker.org

Ben Lomond Quaker Center, P.O. Box 686, Ben Lomond, CA 95005. Phone: (831) 336-8333. Website: www.quakercenter.org

Pendle Hill Conference and Retreat Center, 338 Plush Mill Road, Wallingford, PA 19086, (800) 742-3150, website: www.pendlehill.org

Hinduism

Vedanta Society of Southern California, 1946 Vedanta Place, Hollywood, CA 90068. Phone: (323) 465-7114. Website: www.vedanta.org

Hindu Resources Online. Website: www.hindu.org

Judaism

Metivta Center, 2001 S. Barrington Ave., Suie 106, Los Angeles, CA 90025. Phone: (310) 477-5370. Website: www.metivta.org

N'vay Shalom, 5050 S. Beverly Drive, #534, Beverly Hills, CA 90212. Phone: (213) 463-7728

Maven, Jewish clearinghouse. Website: www.maven.co.il

Kavannah. Website: www.kavannah.org

Chabad. Website: www.chabad.org

Breslov. Website: www.breslov.org

Bnei Baruch Kabbalah. Website: kabbalah-web.org

Virtual Yeshivah/Rasheit Institute for Jewish Spirituality, website: www.rasheit.org

Network of Jewish Renewal Communities. Website: www.jewishrenewal.org

Reform Judaism. Website: www.rj.org/

Conservative Judaism: United Synagogue of Conservative Judaism. Website: www.uscj.org

Islam

ICNA Main Page (Islamic Circle of North America). Website: www.icna.com

Islamic Society of North America. Website: www.isna.net

Al-Islam, website: www.Al-islam.org

Islamic Society of Orange County, 9752 13th St., P.O. Box 1330B, Garden Grove, CA 92844. Phone: (714) 531-1722

Lutheran

Evangelical Lutheran Church of America. Website: www.elca.org

The Pacific Synod of the Evangelical Lutheran Church in America, 23655 Via Del Rio, Yorba Linda, CA 92887. Phone: (714) 692-2791

Science of Mind

Seal Beach Church of Religious Science. Phone: (562) 598-3325

United Church of Religious Science, 3251 W. Sixth St., Los Angeles, CA 90020. Phone: (213) 388-2181. E-mail: sciofmind@aol.com

United Methodist Church

Pathways Network, The Upper Room, P.O. Box 856, Nashville, TN 37202. Phone: (615) 340-7200. Website: www.umc.org/pathways/network

United Methodist Church. Website: www.umc.org

United Methodist Church, 12741 Main St., Garden Grove, CA 92840. Phone: (714) 534-1070

Non-Denominational

Association of Vineyard Churches, 5340 E. La Palma Ave., Anaheim, CA 92807, P.O. Box 17580 Anaheim, CA 92817. Phone: (714) 777-1433. E-mail: info@vineyardusa.org

La Casa de Maria Retreat House, Santa Barbara, CA (personal retreats). Phone: 805-969-5031.

Center for Spiritual Development, 424 S. Batavia St., Santa Ana, CA. Phone: (714) 744-3175

Contemplative Outreach, P.O. Box 737, Butter, NJ 07405. Phone: (973) 838-3384. Website: www.contemplativeoutreach.org

The Mastery Foundation, 1 Charlton Court #104, San Francisco, CA 94123. Phone: (415) 885-8540. Website: www.masteryfoundation.org

Southern California Renewal Communities, 2850 Artesia Blvd., #207, Redondo Beach, CA 90278. Phone: (310) 371-6433

United Religions Initiative, P.O. Box 29242, San Francisco, CA 94129-0242. Phone: (415) 561-2200. Website: www.united-religions.org

Contemplative Outreach Ltd. Website: www.centeringprayer.com

Reading List

Aitken, Robert. *Taking the Path of Zen*. New York: North Point, 1982.

Albom, Mitch. *Tuesdays with Morrie*. New York: Doubleday, 1997.

Armstrong, Karen. *A History of God: the 4,000-Year Quest of Judaism, Christianity and Islam*. (audio) San Francisco: Harper Audio, 1994.

Au, Wilkie, S.J. *By Way of the Heart: Toward a Holistic Christian Spirituality*. New York: Paulist, 1991.

Barry, William A. *God's Passionate Desire: And Our Response*. Notre Dame: Ave Maria Press, 1993.

Barry, William A. *What Do I Want in Prayer*. New York: Paulist, 1994.

Bass, Dorothy C. (editor) *Practicing Our Faith: A Way of Life for a Searching People*. San Francisco: Harper, 1988.

Beck, Charlotte Joko. *Everyday Zen: Love and Work*. San Francisco: Harper, 1989.

_____. *Nothing Special*. San Francisco: Harper, 1993.

Boorstein, Sylvia. *That's Funny, You Don't Look Buddhist: On Being a Faithful Jew and a Passionate Buddhist*. San Francisco: Harper, 1997.

Brueggemann, Walter. *The Prophetic Imagination*. Minneapolis: Fortress, 1978.

Btstam-Dzin-Rgya-Mtsho, His Holiness the Dalai Lama and Thupten Jinpa. *The Four Noble Truths: Fundamentals of the Buddhist Teachings, His Holiness the XIV Dalai Lama*. Lanham, MD: Thorsons, 1998.

Buber, Martin. *I and Thou*. New York: Charles Scribner's Sons, 1970.

_____. *Tales of the Hasidim*. New York: Schocken, 1991.

Cahill, Thomas. *The Gifts of the Jews: How a Tribe of Desert Nomads Changed the Way Everyone Thinks and Feels*. NewYork: Anchor/Doubleday, 1998.

Chodron, Pema. *Start Where You Are: A Guide to Compassionate Living*. Boston: Shambhala, 1994.

_____. *When Things Fall Apart: Heart Advice for Difficult Times*. Boston: Shambhala, 1997.

Cimino, Richard and Don Lattin. *Shopping for Faith: American Religion in the New Millenium*. San Francisco: Jossey-Bass, 1998.

Cooper, Rabbi David. *God is a Verb*. New York: Riverhead, 1997.

_____. *Entering the Sacred Mountain: Exploring the Mystical Practices of Judaism, Buddhism and Sufism*. New York: Crown Publishing, 1995.

Cotter, Jim. *Prayer at Night's Approaching*. Harrisburg, PA: Morehouse, 1998.

Dalai Lama, His Holiness. *Ethics for the New Millenium*. New York: Riverhead, 1999.

Das, Lama Surya. *Awakening to the Sacred: Creating a Spiritual Life from Scratch*. New York: Broadway, 1999.

Dass, Ram. *Still Here: Embracing Aging, Changing, and Dying*. New York: Riverhead, 2000.

De Caussade, Jean-Pierre. *Abandonment to Divine Providence*. New York: Image, 1993.

DeMello, Anthony. *The Way to Love: The Last Meditations of Anthony deMello*. New York: Image, 1995.

Dillard, Annie. *Teaching A Stone to Talk: Expeditions and Encounters*. New York: HarperCollins,1999.

Dogen. Translated by Thomas Cleary. *Shobogenzo: Zen Essays by Dogen*. Honolulu: University of Hawaii, 1992.

Dosick, Rabbi Wayne. *Dancing with God*. San Francisco: HarperSanFrancisco, 1997.

_____. *Living Judaism: The Complete Guide to Jewish Belief, Tradition, and Practice*. San Francisco: HarperSanFrancisco, 1995.

Eck, Diana L. *Encountering God: A Spiritual Journey from Bozeman to Banaras*. Boston: Beacon, 1994.

Elliott, William. *Tying Rocks to Clouds: Meetings and Conversations with Wise and Spiritual People*. New York: Doubleday, 1996.

English, John J. *Spiritual Freedom: From an Experience of the Ignatian Exercises to the Art of Spiritual Guidance*. Chicago: Loyola Press, 1995.

Epstein, Mark. *Thoughts Without a Thinker*. New York: Harper Collins, 1995.

Farnham, Suzanne, Joseph P. Gill and R. Taylor McLean. *Listening Hearts*. Harrisburg, PA: Morehouse, 1991.

Field, Reshad. *The Last Barrier*. Rockport, ME: Element, 1996.

Forbush, W.B. (editor) *Fox's Book of Martyrs*. Zondervan, 1978.

Foster, Richard. *Celebration of Discipline: The Path to Spiritual Growth*. San Francisco: Harper, 1988.

Fox, Matthew. *Meditations with Meister Eckhart*. New York: Crossroad, 1993.

Frankl, Viktor E. *Man's Search for Meaning*. New York: Mass Market, 1998.

Friedman, Maurice. *A Heart of Wisdom: Religion and Human Wholeness*. Albany, NY: State University of New York Press, 1992.

Glassman, Bernard, and Rick Fields. *Instructions to the Cook: A Zen Master's Lessons in Living a Life that Matters*. New York: Bell Tower, 1996.

Glassman, Bernie. *Bearing Witness: A Zen Master's Lessons in Making Peace*. New York: Bell Tower, 1998.

Goldstein, Joseph. *Insight Meditation: The Practice of Freedom*. Boston: Shambhala, 1994.

_____, and Jack Kornfield. *Seeking the Heart of Wisdom*. Boston: Shambhala, 1987.

Gunaratana, Venerable Henepola. *Mindfulness in Plain English*. Somerville, MA: Wisdom, 1991.

Guyon, Madam Jeanne. *Library of Spiritual Classics: Experiencing the Depths of Jesus*

Christ (Volume 2). Augusta, GA: Christian Books, 1999.

Hall, Thelma. *Too Deep for Words: Rediscovering Lectio Divina*. New York: Paulist, 1988.

Hanh, Thich Nhat. *Cultivating the Mind of Love: The Practice of Looking Deeply in the Mahayana Buddhist Tradition*. Berkeley: Parallax, 1996.

_____. *Guide to Walking Meditation*. Norwich, CT: Fellowship of Reconciliation, 1985.

_____. *Living Buddha, Living Christ*. New York: Riverhead Books, 1995.

_____. *Present Moment, Wonderful Moment: Mindfulness Verses for Daily Living*. Berkeley: Parallax, 1990.

_____. *Zen Keys*. New York: Doubleday, 1995.

_____. *Breathe! You are Alive. Sutra on the Full Awareness of Breathing*. Berkeley: Parallax, 1996.

Hays, Edward. *Pray All Ways*. Easton: Forest of Peace, 1981.

_____ *Prayers for the Domestic Church: A Handbook for Worship in the Home*. Easton: Forest of Peace, 1989.

Heschel, Abraham Joshua. *The Sabbath: Its Meaning for Modern Man*. New York: Noonday Press, 1979.

_____. *The Earth is the Lord's: The Inner World of the Jew in Eastern Europe*. Woodstock, VT: Jewish Lights, 1995.

Holmes, Ernest. *How to Live the Science of Mind*. Marina del Rey, CA: DeVorss, 1989.

_____. *The Science of Mind*. New York: Putnam, 1988.

Hughes, Gerard W. *God of Surprises*. Boston: Cowley, 1993.

Hurnard, Hannah. *Hind's Feet on High Places*. Uhrichsville, OH: Barbour, 1998.

James, William. *The Varieties of Religious Experience*. New York: Collier Books, 1961.

Johnson, Robert A. *Inner Work: Using Dreams and Active Imagination for Personal Growth*. San Francisco: HarperSanFrancisco, 1989.

Johnston, William. *The Cloud of Unknowing and the Book of Privy Counseling*. New York: Image, 1996.

Jung, Carl Gustav. Michael Fordham and Herbert Read (editors). *The Collected Works of Carl Jung, No. 11, Psychology and Religion—West and East*. Princeton, NJ: Princeton University Press, 1969.

Kamenetz, Rodger. *The Jew in the Lotus*. San Francisco: HarperSanFrancisco, 1994.

_____. *Stalking Elijah*. San Francisco: HarperSanFrancisco, 1997.

Kaplan, Aryeh. *Jewish Meditation: A Practical Guide*. New York: Schocken, 1995.

_____. *Meditation and the Bible*. York Beach, ME: Samuel Weiser, 1988.

_____. *Meditation and Kabbalah*. York Beach, ME: Samuel Weiser, 1989.

Kapleau, Philip. *The Three Pillars of Zen*. New York: Anchor/Doubleday, 1989.

Keating, Thomas. *Open Mind, Open Heart: The Contemplative Dimension of the Gospel*. Rockport, ME: Element, 1994.

Kelly, Thomas R. and Richard J. Foster. *A Testament of Devotion*. San Francisco: HarperSanFrancisco, 1996.

Kelsey, Morton T. *Adventure Inward: Christian Growth Through Personal Journal Writing*. Minneapolis: Augsberg, 1980.

Kornfeld, Jack. *A Path with Heart*. New York: Bantam, 1993.

Krishnamurti, J. *Freedom from the Known*. San Francisco: Harper, 1969.

Labowitz, Shoni. *Miraculous Living: A Guided Journey in Kabbalah Through the Ten Gates of the Tree of Life*. New York: Simon & Schuster, 1998.

L'Engle, Madeleine. *Walking on Water: Reflections on Faith and Art*. Wheaton, IL: Harold Shaw Publishers, 1980.

Levine, Stephen. *Who Dies?* New York: Doubleday, 1982.

Linn, Dennis, Sheila Fabricant Linn and Matthew Linn. *Sleeping with Bread: Holding What Gives You Life*. New York: Paulist, 1995.

Linzer, Judith. *Torah and Dharma: Jewish Seekers in Eastern Religions*. Northvale, NJ: Jason Aronson, 1996.

Long, Philomene. *American Zen Bones: Maezumi Roshi Stories*. Venice, CA: Beyond Baroque,1999.

Loori, John Daido. *The Eight Gates of Zen*. New York: Dharma Communications, 1992.

_____. *The Heart of Being: Moral and Ethical Teachings of Zen Buddhism*. Boston: Tuttle, 1996.

Loring, Patricia. *Listening Spirituality, Vol. 1: Personal Spiritual Practices Among Friends*. Washington, DC: Openings, 1997.

Manning, Brennan. *Abba's Child: The Cry of the Heart for Intimate Belonging*. Colorado Springs, CO: NavPress, 1994.

Matt, Daniel. *The Essential Kabbalah: The Heart of Jewish Mysticism*. San Francisco: HarperCollins, 1996.

May, Gerald G. *Will and Spirit: A Contemplative Psychology*. San Francisco: Harper, 1987.

McLaren, Brian. *Finding Faith: A Self-Discovery Guide for Your Spiritual Quest*. New York: Zondervan, 1999.

Merton, Thomas. *The Ascent to Truth*. New York: Harcourt Brace, 1989.

Mitchell, Stephen. *Tao Te Ching: A New English Version*. San Francisco: Harper Perennial, 1992.

Mitroff, Ian I. and Elizabeth A. Denton. *A Spiritual Audit of Corporate America: A Hard Look at Spirituality, Religion, and Values in the Workplace*. San Francisco: Jossey-Bass, 1999.

Mulholland, M. Robert. *Invitation to a Journey: A Road Map for Spiritual Formation*. Dowers, IL: Intervarsity, 1993.

Neng, Hui. Thomas Cleary (translator). *The Sutra of Hui Neng: Grans Master of Zen* Boston: Shambhala, 1998.

Norris, Kathleen. *Dakota: A Spiritual Geography*. Boston: Houghton Mifflin, 1993.

_____. *The Cloister Walk*. New York: Riverhead Books, 1996.

_____. *Amazing Grace: A Vocabulary of Faith*. New York: Riverhead, 1999.

Nouwen, Henri J.M. *Reaching Out: The Three Movements of the Spiritual Life*. New York: Image, 1986.

_____. *The Return of the Prodigal Son*. New York: Image/Doubleday, 1992.

_____. *With Open Hands*. Notre Dame, IN: Ave Maria, 1995.

_____. *Here and Now: Living in the Spirit*. New York: Crossroad, 1994.

Payne, Leanne. *The Healing Presence: Curing the Soul through Union with Christ*. New York: Baker, 1995.

Pennington, Basil, Moran, Michael, and Kushner, Lawrence. *Centered Living: The Way of Centering Prayer*. New York: Image, 1988.

Phillips, J. B. *Your God is Too Small*. New York: MacMillan, 1997.

Prager, Dennis. *Happiness is a Serious Problem: A Human Nature Repair Manual*. New York: Harper Collins, 1998.

Price, John Randolph. *A Spiritual Philosophy for the New World: The 60-Day Non-Human Program to Rise Above the Ego*. Boerne, TX: Quartus, 1997.

Rohr, Richard. *Everything Belongs*. New York: Crossroad, 1999.

Russell, A. J. *God Calling*. Wunickville: Barbour, 1989

St. Teresa of Avila. *Life of Saint Teresa of Avila by Herself*. London: Penguin, 1988.

_____. *The Way of Perfection*. New York: Image, 1991.

Salwalk, Dale. *Wonders of Solitude*. Novato: New World Library, 1998.

Schwartz, Tony. *What Really Matters: Searching for Wisdom in America*. New York: Bantam Books, 1995.

Sells, Michael, *Approaching the Qur'án: The Early Revelations*. Ashland, OR: White Cloud Press, 1999.

Shainberg, Lawrence. *Ambivalent Zen: One Man's Adventures on the Dharma Path*. New York: Vintage, 1997

Shapira, Rabbi Kalonymus Kalman. *Conscious Community: A Guide to Inner Work*. Northvale, NJ: Jason Aronson, 1996.

Sims, Bennett J. *Servanthood: Leadership for the Third Millenium*. Cambridge: Cowley, 1997.

Sinetar, Marsha. *Ordinary People As Monks and Mystics*. New York: Paulist Press, 1986.

Smith, Huston. *Forgotten Truth: The Common Vision of the World's Religions*. San Francisco: Harper, 1992.

_____. *The World's Religions*. San Francisco: Harper, 1991.

_____. *Why Religion Matters*. San Francisco: HarperSanFrancisco, 2001.

Suzuki, Shunryu. *Zen Mind, Beginner's Mind*. New York: Weatherhill, 1995.

Tozer, A.W. *The Knowledge of the Holy: The Attributes of God: Their Meaning the Christian Life*. San Francisco: Harper, 1978.

Tworkov, Helen. *Zen in America*. New York: Kodansha, 1994.

Underhill, Evelyn and Grace A. Brame. *The Ways of the Spirit*. New York: Crossroad, 1993.

Underhill, Evelyn. *Mysticism: Seeing the Holy in the Ordinary*. San Francisco: Harper, 1995.

Underhill, Evelyn. *Mystics of the Church*. Harrisburg, PA: Morehouse-Barlow, 1988.

Van Steere, Douglas and Timothy Jones. *Dimensions of Prayer: Cultivating a Relationship with God*. Nashville: Upper Room, 1997.

Vrajaprana, Pravrajika (editor). *Living Wisdom: Vedanta in the West*. Hollywood: Vedanta Press, 1994.

_____. *Vedanta: A Simple Introduction*. Hollywood: Vedanta Press, 1999.

Walsch, Neale Donald. *Conversations with God: An Uncommon Dialogue, Book 1*. New York: Putnam, 1996.

Wiederkehr, Macrina. *A Tree Full of Angels: the Nature and Development of Spiritual Consciousness*. San Francisco: Harper, 1995.

Wilber, Ken. *A Brief History of Everything*. Boston: Shambhala, 1996.

_____. *Grace and Grit. Spirituality and Healing in the Life and Death of Treya Killam Wilber*. Boston: Shambhala, 1993.

_____. *No Boundary: Eastern and Western Approaches to Personal Growth*. Boston: Shambhala, 1985.

Willard, Dallas. *The Divine Conspiracy: Rediscovering our Hidden Life in God*. San Francisco: Harper, 1998.

Wolff, Pierre. *Discernment: The Art of Choosing Well*. Ligouri, MO: Ligouri Publications. 1993.

Wuellner, Flora Slosson. *Prayer and Our Bodies*. Nashville: Abingdon, 1987.

Zaleski, Philip and Paul Kaufman. *Gifts of the Spirit: Living the Wisdom of the Great Religious Traditions*. San Francisco: HarperSanFrancisco, 1997.

Zopa Rinpoche, Lama. *Transforming Problems into Happiness*. Boston: Wisdom, 1993.

Zweig, Connie and Jeremiah Abrams. *Meeting the Shadow: The Hidden Power of the Dark Side Of Human Nature*. New York: Tarcher, 1990.